How to Live from Your Heart

Attract Loving Relationships, Access Your Innate Creativity, and Overcome Blocks to Claiming Happiness

Nanette V. Hucknall

self-help general
self-help personal growth happiness
philosophy general

Copyright 2016 by MSI Press, LLC

For information, contact
MSI Press
1760-F Airline Highway, #203
Hollister, CA 95023

Cover design by Carl Leaver

Library of Congress Control Number 2016935315

ISBN: 978-1-942891-24-6

Dedication

I dedicate this book to my teachers RHH, and MM,
And to Lord Jesus whose teaching about
the power of the heart inspired this book.

Contents

Acknowledgements

My thanks goes to:

First and most important, Betty Leaver, the managing editor, who was most helpful at all times and a very professional, pleasant woman to work with.

To the copy editor, Mary Ann Raemisch, who did a good job with a tight schedule.

To Olga Denisko, who edited the material as it was developed and gave me insightful suggestions around some of the content.

To Kathy Crowe, who is always there to help me in my work. She has been more than instrumental in making this book become a reality.

And to Carl Leaver for designing the beautiful cover.

Introduction

Buddha said: The way is not in the sky. The way is in the heart.

Living from your heart is a way of life. It means to listen with your heart, to relate to others with your heart, to receive and give to others with your heart, to access knowledge with your heart, to inspire and be inspired, and to learn discrimination, trusting in your heart's ability to recognize right from wrong. It means being open to any possibility and any creative thought.

The heart is the way to higher wisdom and the spirit within. Using your heart as an instrument brings an acceptance of nature's beauty, the containment of opposites and a way for healing energies to flow.

But what is the heart? The physical heart, of course, is an organ that keeps us alive, but the physical heart is very different from the heart this book is referring to. Where does one feel love or pain? It always comes not from the physical heart but from a place in the center of our chest. This center, or heart chakra (a Sanskrit Indian term), is a chalice from which all the emotions pour forth. It also contains heart energy, an energy that, when properly directed, nourishes others as well as oneself.

To open the heart to every possibility requires concentration and continuous self-exploration. With an open heart comes the responsibility of its proper use, a responsibility that is sometimes abused. Most religions emphasize relationship—relationship to God, relationship to man. They find relationship important for well-being and the growth of the spirit, but many leaders have fallen because of their misuse of relationship. I refer here to the spiritual teachers who have misused the heart by manipulating others. Many of these spiritual teachers have, in fact, developed and opened the heart by working spiritually on their chosen path before succumbing to personal desires. This false use of the heart happens in exoteric as well as esoteric religions.

The use of the heart is a very powerful tool, and if not used properly, it can cause a lot of unhappiness for the person who is under its spell. I use the word 'spell' literally. The quality of an open heart is very hypnotic. When you experience love coming from a person's heart, it often hides what is being said or being asked for.

One of the functions of the heart center is to connect to the Higher Self, which is part of everyone. It has access to higher wisdom and contains all the good, refined, beautiful qualities a person has accumulated on the path of life's journey. The Higher Self is often represented as a wise being: a woman, a man, or even a light form. This wise being guides the individual through the heart and helps the spirit to blossom. It is spoken of in psychological models as being the part within that understands what is right for the individual.

The willingness to accept change, to learn, to expand one's viewpoint, and to explore and embrace the unknown, are directed by the Higher Self. It also contains the positive traits or characteristics a person displays to others. The ability to love, share, exchange, and cooperate are aspects of this.

With the use of the heart, relationships feel nurtured and dynamic. There develops an inner understanding that helps relationships grow and prosper. This ability expands beyond personal relationships to a broadened understanding of community and diverse cultures. The heart gives an unbiased perspective of world events, one based on justice.

With constant use, the heart becomes a vehicle for learning. It helps in discriminating good and negative action, as well as what is correct behavior.

With the use of the heart comes a feeling of being one with nature. Nature has within it all the aspects that are found in working with the heart. The flowers of a garden represent a person's heart center. When the flowers are in bloom, it's as if the center has opened and the true value or worth of an individual is an open view to everyone. Nature reminds us of what lies within.

Constant use of the heart brings spiritual growth. Without this energy, the individual is walking in a world of finite objects with no hope for change or growth. The disillusions of life are but these finite realities, unchanging and stagnant. With the use of the heart, these disillusions take on a different reality. They are viewed as learning experiences and paths to greater understanding, not only of oneself but also of others. These experiences reflect on the consciousness and can either affect it in a positive or a negative manner.

Some people feel that using the heart will make them appear maudlin or super sweet. This is a mistaken concept. People who act that way are not using their hearts. They are more involved in emotions and needs, which are very different. When people express themselves with their hearts, the quality is often subtle, not obvious. It is an energy that is quiet and refined, yet all encompassing. It's like sitting in a tub of warm water and allowing the warmth to penetrate your whole body. Such warmth is soft and nurturing, not full of need. The energy is not always apparent. The receiver has to be open and receive it without fear or resistance; otherwise it can dissolve into the air.

When I speak of heart energy, I refer to an energy coming through the heart center from a Higher Source that is always loving and wise. Using this type of energy is very different from using psychic energy, which is the energy force of the body. The higher energy only comes through the heart center and is strictly regulated by the heart. An imbalance happens when people force the energy with their will and use it improperly. To avoid any possibility of this occurring, throughout the book I recommend connecting to the Higher Self and letting it guide you.

I have included many exercises in the book to help you use your heart in everyday life. These exercises should be done in sequence. I also suggest methods of application and time frames. Try to follow these, but feel free to add new exercises and experiment. The heart is always the regulator; so follow its indications as to what is best for you.

The exercises are just an introduction to the use of the heart. With each exercise, there is an explanation of what some of the results may be. Again, feel free to not accept that which doesn't work for you.

There are several exercises that will help you link with your Higher Self, and they are listed at the end of the book for you to try.

I would suggest that you begin the book by doing these exercises. Try all of them, one at a time, on separate days. Pick the one that you feel most comfortable doing and which gives you the best results. The main thing that needs to be emphasized is that the connection to the Higher Self is always through the heart. If you work with the exercises on a regular basis, eventually you can let go of the exercises, and just with your heart immediately establish the link to the Higher Self and its guidance. Like anything important in life, it takes practice. So when you start to work with the exercises, don't feel discouraged if you don't experience the Higher Self immediately. It's true that in time you will, but sometimes you almost have to demand its attention, particularly when you have never done this kind of work before.

The beauty of the heart is its ability for diversity and its acceptance of anything new. Be open to its energy and try to feel the beauty of its qualities.

Note: I use "he" in odd numbered chapters and "she" in even numbered chapters, but the material is meant for both genders. I use the word disidentifiy and disidentified throughout the book. It means looking at something from a place of observation. It does not mean being disinterested.

Part One: Defining the Heart Center

Understanding the Heart

Imagine yourself in a deeply loving and completely fulfilling relationship, excited by each new day. Imagine you awake to intellectually stimulating work that matters in the world. Picture the deepest longings in your heart blooming into real, tangible manifestations of your creativity. You can have all of this. You already have the road map and the knowledge to create this beautiful life, and all that wisdom resides in your heart. Your heart knows:

- Right from wrong
- Creativity from procrastination
- Love from lust
- Joy from mania
- Honesty from falsehoods

And more.

And here's the best news. Tapping into your heart communications skills will:

- Bring you a deeper perspective on events in your own life and in the world
- Help you attain and retain emotional balance

- Unleash your creativity and make it easier to tap into throughout your day
- Bring awareness to your own gifts
- Help you develop deeper, more fulfilling relationships with others
- Access your innate intuitive guidance
- Connect you to higher wisdom

To understand your heart is to understand how to work with energies. These energies flow through you and affect your personality, as well as the way you relate to others. Understanding heart energy is learning how to make these energies work for you in a positive manner, a manner that will help you to grow morally and spiritually and help you in your relationships with others.

There have been many schools, from the psychological to the religious and philosophical, that speak of the power of love, the power of the spiritual self, and the power of higher inspiration. All of these are energies flowing through the heart center.

The heart center is an instrument that literally expresses these qualities. As with any instrument, it is necessary to practice in order to bring forth its finest sound. It takes time, dedication, and knowledge to make this happen. It is up to you to do the work, to want to use your heart, and to have the need for an open heart full of compassion and understanding.

Having an open heart will change your behavior and affect those who are close to you.

With the use of your heart, you can develop the means to have lasting relationships and an abundance of energy, and you can even discover your creative self. All of this is part of everyone's potential, a potential seldom used to its fullest.

First, it is necessary to come to a better understanding of your heart center. Emotions always flow through this center, which is located in the middle of your chest in line with the physical heart. Emotion usually causes a pressure or a knot in this center. If it is a loving feeling, the pressure is often accompanied by warmth and expansion. The saying, "I feel my heart is going to burst" reflects this expansion. The saying, "I feel my heart is going to break" reflects what happens when the energy in this center becomes contracted, causing a real pain.

Neither of the above comes from the physical heart. There are energy centers throughout the body, which are repositories of psychic energy, the life energy flowing through a person's physical body. This energy vibrates through the organs and the vascular and nervous systems of the body, leaving only at death.

This same energy literally activates physical sensations and causes them to affect the mental and emotional makeup of a person.

This energy is also an activating force in the centers. It varies depending on the use of each center. If a person never uses the heart center, then it will not be activated. Such a person would be cold and distant, someone who has a difficult time relating to others.

When someone uses his heart center, that person will emit warmth and gentleness. Meeting someone like this may make you say, "This person has a good heart," meaning an open-heart center.

With the use of your heart, feelings deepen, and they can create a better understanding of others. Look at those people you feel are loving and caring. Their openness and acceptance is usually a quality that is very apparent. This same openness allows you to be responsive and warm, which causes your heart to expand a little in return. When this type of exchange takes place, it is truly communication in its best sense.

It is easy to use your heart with someone who is like this. It is naturally much harder with a relationship that is more distant. Unfortunately, most people will neglect trying to use their heart with someone who is detached and aloof. Yet sending such a person the warmth of your heart can open him up and help him, in turn, awaken his own heart.

Part of increasing the awareness of using your heart is simply to use it in every situation, whether or not it is comfortable. Such a practice not only will help you to see the truth behind what is happening, but also will provide a means to change your own negative behavior habits.

The following story illustrates this:

> There was once upon a time a very great Raja in India who owned an enormous kingdom full of abundance and wealth. This Raja spent most of his time in his palace being entertained by his many wives. One day, a very wise sage came to the palace and asked to see the Raja.
>
> The Raja invited him to a dinner party he was giving that evening. During the dinner, the Raja asked the sage to talk about his practical teaching. The sage

replied, "I teach a very special type of yoga, a yoga that is only for a select few."

Of course, this aroused the curiosity of the Raja, and he asked the sage if he would teach him this special yoga. The sage told the Raja that he would be happy to take him as a student if the Raja would first do him a favor.

The Raja agreed, not thinking that it was anything he could not fulfill. The sage then requested, "Please give me a piece of your heart."

The Raja was aghast at such a request. "If I gave you a piece of my heart, I would die!"

The sage just laughed and said, "You promised, and I hold you to your word. I will return in a week."

The Raja became very angry that the sage had tricked him. He felt foolish for having agreed without hearing the request first. Since his other guests had heard him agree, his code of honor was now in jeopardy. What a dilemma! How was he to retain his honor and not give up his life?

The Raja called in all the wise men in his kingdom and asked their advice. They all made suggestions, but none fulfilled the original request. A week went by quickly and the sage returned.

"Well, are you ready to give me a piece of your heart?" demanded the sage.

"How cruel you are! I have heard you are a man full of love and compassion. How can you ask me to kill myself?" replied the Raja.

"I asked you for a piece of your heart. I did not ask you to kill yourself. You can do this request without dying. I give you one more week to honor your agreement."

The Raja was now really confused. How could he give him a piece of his heart without dying? Again, he sought the advice of all the learned men in his realm. No one seemed to know the answer. Feeling more and more depressed, the Raja went to his private chapel to pray. While he was praying, a voice said to him, "The answer lies in your heart."

The Raja then asked his heart for help. He felt an answer come from it. His heart said, "Look into the sage's eyes and ask him to first give you a piece of his heart."

The next week, the sage returned and the Raja looked deeply into his eyes and asked the question. As he looked, he saw the sage's eyes deepen and fill with warmth. The Raja felt the warmth of the sage's eyes fill his own chest with energy so intense his heart vibrated. It was so strong and loving he could barely contain it.

"Now that you have received a piece of my heart, can you do the same?"

"No, I don't know how. Please teach me." The Raja humbly bowed down.

The sage smiled, "Now I will accept you as my student."

This story illustrates how the heart is pure energy, energy that can be given to others in a positive way.

Really understanding the true meaning of nature and man's relationship to it is also part of developing the heart. If you are in tune with nature, you will find yourself experiencing a heightened awareness of its hidden mysteries, mysteries inherent in all of life. It will help you begin to realize your own creative self. The freedom of the spirit comes with this deeper understanding.

Wisdom comes through the heart, not through the mind. The mind only processes it. The essence and depth of understanding is developed through the heart center.

Too often, someone will use his heart indiscriminately and seduce another person with its energy. This is a misuse of energy. An example is projecting love onto someone who mistakes it for personal love and becomes hurt as a consequence. Therefore, in using the heart, there needs to be a sense of responsibility. It is necessary to establish ethical practices; otherwise, the heart will close.

With the use of the heart comes a strong desire to help others. Again, it has to be done with discrimination; otherwise, you may be interfering with another person's life. The need to help is always very positive, but the need may be coming only from you, not the other person. First, it is important to be certain that the person you want to help really wants help. Often this is not the case, even in the worst situations. It's best to always ask. When you ask, be aware if the answer is coming from the person's heart. If it is, then it's a true answer. Someone may not want to hurt your feelings by refusing, so you should try to make the offer loose enough that the person can easily say no.

The heart is used to regulate feelings. It is important to recognize the source of these energies and how they operate through the heart. To begin with, the heart is like a fine tuning fork. It is sensitive to every feeling and picks up on hidden feelings. The more you use it in relating to others, the more sensitive it becomes. Every time you use your heart, it becomes more capable of discerning correctly. This discernment is essential if you are to work with your heart in relationships. In other words, the more you discover the hidden meaning of what someone says, the easier it becomes to discover the truth.

With each effort to use the heart there is a definite feeling of attunement. This attunement is an energy flowing through the heart from a source called "the archetypal wise person," or what is referred to in this book as the Higher Self.

The enlightened part of your unconscious has the understanding and discernment to know the proper way to behave in any situation. This part is always geared to you and your personal process. For example, if you are thinking of changing your job and you have two job offers and can't decide which one to take, the Higher Self can look at both situations and determine the best one for you. This advice can flow through your heart in an intuitive feeling of knowing, or it can be a literal knowing that comes through your mind.

When you use your heart for understanding, it is a different process from using your mind. For example, when you use your mind to decide a given question, you simply think about it and decide. To use your heart, take the question and imagine placing it into your heart. Let the question go, and then wait for the answer to come either from your mind or from an inner feeling. The answer will be much deeper, taking in many more factors, when it comes from your heart.

The following is an exercise to get in touch with your heart center. Before doing this, think of a question you want to put in your heart.

Exercise:

> *Find a quiet place where you will be undisturbed. Sit comfortably. If you are sitting in a chair, have your legs straight in front of you, or if you are sitting on a pillow in yoga fashion, cross your legs in front of you.*
>
> *Close your eyes and take some deep breaths. As you breathe, try to let go of any thoughts or feelings, resting your mind and body, feeling yourself relax into a peaceful state.*
>
> *Next, concentrate and focus your mind on your heart center, which is situated in the middle of your chest.*
>
> *Keep concentrating on the center and try to experience it. You may feel a slight pressure or warmth, or even a movement or expansion, or you may see a light. When you experience something, you know you are connected to it.*
>
> *At that time, you can place your question into the center and let it go.*
>
> *The answer may come right away in a feeling or a thought, or it may come later when you are walking down the street, or even in a dream state. Keep placing the question into your heart center until you feel it has been answered. Sometimes the answer will come in the form of another question, a question that goes a little deeper. Take this question and work with it in the same manner.*

Often a person will get a significant answer but they feel it may be too simple. This is because our western conditioning complicates us. We feel simple solutions should be more complex. Yet, the simpler a solution, the easier it can be understood and the easier it is to fulfill.

Exercise:

> *Close your eyes and take some deep breaths. As you breathe, try to let go of any thoughts or feelings, resting your mind and body, feeling yourself relax into a peaceful state.*
>
> *Think of a problem you need answered.*

First, take the problem and think about it with your mind. Analyze it and come to a solution that your mind feels is correct. Write down your thoughts.
Again, close your eyes, relax your body and breathe deeply.
Next, take the same problem, focus on your heart center and imagine placing the problem into your heart center. Concentrate on the problem only and let it go. Wait for some kind of answer, and notice if the answer is the same or different from your mind's answer. Write it down.
Next, take your heart's answer back to your mind and think about it again, and then take that conclusion back to your heart. Keep doing this process until you feel you have a good answer and it is complete. Write as you do this.

When you work with your heart, answers will become deeper. With each exercise you do, you should experience the heart center in the same manner as with the first exercise. If you experienced it as a slight pressure, make certain you feel the slight pressure again when you continue putting questions into it. It is important to keep the connection clear and strong. The connection will become stronger the more you work with it.

Understanding the functions of the heart center is the first step to opening it. The more you work with it, the more it will open, slowly, and in that opening you will feel the energy which is there more deeply, an energy full of love, compassion, understanding, and wisdom. Work with your heart daily, and it will become not just a part of you, but also the main instrument you have for dealing with life and all its happenings.

Remember to use your heart in all your relationships. It will deepen not only those relationships, but also your inner knowledge concerning them.

Exercise:

Close your eyes, relax your body, breathe deeply and go through the previous process of connecting with your heart center.
Think about someone you know who is having difficulties. Put that person's name in your heart and ask to be given information on how you can help that person.

If the answer feels right to you, try to follow it.
The heart is the key to spiritual growth. It will always lead you correctly and give you the knowledge needed to confront life and all that it brings.

2

Making the Heart Work for You

Each person has a unique way to access and experience the heart center. You may be a person who feels pressure in your chest. This pressure tells you that your heart center is being activated. You may also experience a charge of energy that feels like a sudden wave of heat or an expansion of the chest. These are common ways in which people experience their heart center.

Some other ways that are less common are a sudden quickening of breath that resounds in the middle of your chest, a fast or slow movement in the same area that can feel like a rotating ball, a sharp pain that lasts just an instant, or a wave of oscillating colors. You may even see a symbol. A rose or a flame is a common symbol for the heart.

People experience and process information in four different ways:

Visual: You can close your eyes and see a scene with the mind's eye. If you are visual, you can literally see scenes and sometimes they will be moving. You may see color or symbols when you connect to your heart.

Auditory: You can hear from a place inside you. You may hear voices or even music. Beethoven wrote everything with his inner ear after he went deaf. He could hear it perfectly, even the orchestral arrangements. You may experience sound, or even a silent 'yes' when working with your heart.

Sensory: You experience everything in your body. You feel definite body reactions to emotional situations. For example, if someone is criticizing you, you may feel sudden tension and constriction in parts of your body. In connecting with your heart, you would probably feel a negative reaction in your chest.

Feeling: These people have an emotional response. Your reaction to things is usually feeling them, whether it be feeling a person's moods or just feeling your own emotions fully. You would probably feel warmth when you connect to your heart center.

The above are the standard ways of human experience. Of course, no one person has just one of these modalities. Humans, in their complexity, make many combinations and even change them for certain situations. Generally, there are two you will find most prominent, and even those will vary in intensity according to your personal responsiveness.

Exercise:

> *Close your eyes and take some deep breaths. When you feel you are calm, imagine the following:*
> *You go into your kitchen and walk over to the refrigerator. You open the door and open your vegetable tray. You take out a lemon. You close the tray and slam the refrigerator door. Next, you walk to your counter and take a knife from the drawer and slice the lemon. You pick up the lemon and suck it. Just as you do that, a cat jumps up on the counter and grabs the lemon.*

In analyzing this, if you can clearly see the scene of your kitchen, you are a visual person. If you can experience the slamming of the refrigerator door, you would be auditory. Of course, tasting the bitterness of the lemon would make you a sensory person, and feeling emotion when the cat jumps up would be a clue that you are a feeling person.

Again, these are generalizations, and in some circumstance you may experience the effects you are not attuned to. Once you have determined the ways in which you experience things, it would be interesting to experiment with the other ways. It's also fun to share this information with others and help them determine their ways of knowing.

With each of these modalities, there are some definite recurring themes. For example, when you link with your heart and feel pressure, you will know pressure in that area means your heart is activating. When this happens during a conversation with someone, you will know that the person or the subject matter is something that is very important to you. The same is true with the other modes. You may sense or see a color between you and the other person, or you may feel warmth or even coldness flowing from your heart toward her. When you are connected, the inner ear may send you quiet messages. The main thing is to try to be aware of your heart's activity.

During my therapy work I sometimes work with the Higher Self to find answers or direction for the client. I often work with these modalities as indicators, which clearly come from the Higher Self.

Tom, a client who was working with his heart center to determine what area of vocation he needed to pursue, had an experience of first linking with his heart center and feeling it as a pressure. Since he was strongly connected to his body and was a sensory person, I asked his Higher Self to give him a body response for a "yes" answer. The response was a very strong twitching in his left eye. I then asked for a "no" signal, and the response was the same strong twitching, but in his right eye. A "maybe" signal was both eyes twitching. I used this method to ask his Higher Self questions that would help him.

With another client, Julie, who was very visual, her Higher Self showed her colors for signals. She saw brilliant yellow for "yes," a gray color for "no," and dirty ochre for "maybe."

The other modes work just as well. An auditory person will actually hear the Higher Self, and the feeling person will usually have warm and cold emotional responses. Sometimes there will be a combination.

As you use your heart, the ways in which you experience it will become stronger, so there will come a time when you can feel it as a living part of you, a part that can contain the positive as well as the negative emotions.

There are some very important methods with which you can exercise the heart center. Exercising the heart center is the same as exercising a muscle. The more you use it, the stronger it becomes, and, like a muscle, it actually grows bigger in size. Thus, the saying, "That person has a big heart," can be taken literally. With exercise, the heart expands into a very strong vessel, one that has the ability to hold energies coming from within or energies from outside sources. These energies vary in degree and vibration. Using your heart helps you to actually feel the energy flow and know how to use it in a positive manner.

Many of the exercises in this chapter will help you begin strengthening your heart center and even begin the slow process of opening your heart.

It is very important not to force this center to open. Forcing it will cause an imbalance that will affect other parts of your body. There are other centers that need to be regulated with the heart, and forcing the heart will hurt the normal flow of energy that is dispersed. Taking any one of the exercises and overdoing it would be forcing. Each of these exercises should be done one at a time, and never more than once a day. If in doubt about overuse, it is best to stop for a while before resuming the practices.

The heart center is a delicate instrument that needs fine-tuning. Like any instrument, it has to be well taken care of. Protect it when you are tired, cradle it when you feel upset, and hold it when you need sustenance. Like an instrument, the heart has the most beautiful vibrations, and like an instrument, it needs to be played by an expert, someone who understands and knows its qualities.

These exercises will help train you to become an expert. Doing them slowly and carefully will make you a skilled player and hopefully will enhance your spiritual nature.

Using your heart can only bring you closer to the inner world of the spirit, nature, humankind, and the true meaning of God or the Source. Many teachers have sent the message, "Love one another." Making that happen is not an easy task. So remember, working with your heart is a slow process of deep learning.

The following are exercises that will help you to begin strengthening your heart. With all of these exercises, begin by finding a quiet spot that is comfortable. Close your eyes and breathe deeply, and with each breath, let go of any thoughts or emotions. Then, when you feel you are in a peaceful place within, focus all your attention on your heart center until you experience it. These exercises should be practiced for only three minutes at a time and should be done one at a time. Practice the first one for two weeks, then go to the next one for two weeks, etc.

Exercise One:

> Go to Chapter One and repeat the initial exercise of
> connecting to your heart center. Concentrate on the way
> in which you are experiencing your heart, and as you
> concentrate, try slowly to help the energy grow stronger.
> You do this by asking your Higher Self to be with you
> and to help make this happen. If, for example, you feel
> a pressure, ask that the pressure become stronger, or,
> if you see a light, ask that the light become larger, etc.

*Keep concentrating and asking until the strengthening
happens. Again, let it get stronger, but don't overdo it.*

Another way of doing this is, when you feel you are experiencing your heart center, begin to breathe deeply and with each exhaling of breath, feel your heart center grow bigger. Do this particular exercise for only one minute at a time.

Exercise Two:

*In this exercise, take the way in which you experience
your heart center and make the energy stronger, then
ask that it lessen slowly back down to nothing. Repeat
this three times.*

The purpose of doing this is for you to learn how to regulate your heart. If, for instance, you experience a peaceful place within and if, then, your heart center becomes over activated, it will detract from the peaceful feeling. This exercise teaches you how you can lessen the intensity without shutting down your connection.

Don't be discouraged if you can't do this right away. It does take practice. When you feel you have experienced your heart physically, you can start doing some exercises to help you utilize your heart's potential.

Exercise Three:

*Go through the process of connecting with your heart
center.
Take a question or a problem and use your mind to
focus on it, then place it into your heart center and ask
for an answer or further clarification. Let the question
go and try to stay centered in your heart until a thought
or a feeling or an image arises.*

Write anything down that comes up for you around the question. You may also experience nothing at the time, but later when you are doing something else, a clear thought may come in that answers the question. Try doing this every day for just five or ten minutes. The answers may be cloudy at first, so give it time. Remember, you are opening up something new and it needs training. When you start to get answers, the answers should be clear. If they are cloudy, your own wishful thinking may come in, so ask the question again.

Part of using your heart is using it in relating to others. A later chapter focuses on how to work with your heart in relationships, but for now, you can do the following exercise to start working with it.

Exercise Four:

> *When you are with someone, connect to your heart center by focusing your mind on it. Then, think of linking your heart to the other person's heart. This should help you understand clearly what the person is saying.*

Often, words do not express a person's true feelings.

You can practice exercises three and four on a regular basis. They will help you to begin using your heart daily.

The following is a story about someone using his heart for the first time. It illustrates what not to do:

> Once upon a time, in ancient Cambodia, there was a wise man living in a cave in the mountains. A young man named Eshar came to the wise man and asked him to teach him how to open his heart because he wanted to be able to truly love.
>
> The wise man told the boy to go into the village and use his heart with the very first person he met. He was to ask the person to give him something to eat. If the person refused to do so, Eshar should do the same with the next person, and so on. Once Eshar was given something to eat, he should thank the person and consciously feel gratitude in his heart.
>
> Eshar left for the town, and on the way, he met an old man who was pulling a cart loaded with bundles. It was very hot, and the old man could barely walk with the heat and the heavy load he was pulling. He stopped when the youth approached him, and when he heard Eshar's request he replied, "I'm sorry, I haven't anything to give you. I've just been evicted from my home and have no food or dwelling to go to."
>
> The youth waved good-bye and continued on his way. Next, he met a young woman who was running, carrying a crying baby in her arms. The boy again asked for food and the girl looked at him as if he were

crazy. "My baby is sick and I have to find a doctor," she said, and kept running down the road toward the village.

All the people Eshar met were deep into their own troubles and had no food for him. Finally, he entered the village and approached a rich man who threw him a coin to buy food. Eshar sat down and tried to feel gratitude in his heart for the coin. Nothing happened. He tried and tried, and finally, disappointed, he fell asleep.

In his sleep, the wise man appeared and, taking his hand, showed him the burdened old man and said, "If you had used your heart, you would have felt compassion for him and would have offered to help him."

Next, he was shown the woman and baby. "She needed you to run faster with the baby to the doctor. If you had used your heart, you would have known that."

The wise man showed Eshar each person he had met until, finally, Eshar saw the rich man who had thrown him the coin.

"This man only needed a thank you," he explained. "The heart's gratitude is for those who truly give. All of those people you met would have felt this toward you, if you had used your heart to help them."

Eshar protested, "But you told me to ask for food!"

"I told you to use your heart first. If you had done so, you would have forgotten about asking for food," answered the teacher.

When you start to work with your heart center, you will be amazed at how many functions it has. The ones you may be familiar with are:

- Giving love
- Compassion
- Intuition
- Feeling emotions, both positive and negative

The less familiar functions are:

- The ability to mirror others (listening with the heart)
- Inspiration and creativity
- The instrument for healing energy
- The source of higher wisdom (the Higher Self)
- A conduit to the mind
- The way to deepen your spirit
- Discrimination
- Finding inner peace

The heart is the vehicle for all of the above energies. As you refine your vehicle, it can hold, and give out, more and more energy. It's like filling a glass with water. The bigger the glass, the more water it can hold. If the glass is thin, it's more likely to break than a glass that is thick and solid.

3

Heart Energy – What is it?

Heart energy flows through the heart from a source in the universe. Different religious sects label this source according to their belief systems. It can be called God, Brahma, Shiva, The Divine Mother, etc.

Essentially, this energy comes from a Higher Source and passes through several stages before reaching an individual. It flows through the heart center in waves, very much like solar energy. These waves of energy change as they pass through the heart. They vary according to the makeup of the individual and also in the way that the individual uses them.

With each use of the heart, these waves become stronger and purer. They vibrate in the heart center and affect others. Again, this energy is as strong as the individual's capacity to contain it and use it.

The heart that is activated with this energy uses it for its many functions. The energy will vary in intensity according to the function. For example, if you are sending love energy to a friend, you will use a stronger amount of energy than if you are using heart energy to answer a personal question. When the energy goes outward, it has to be more intense in order to reach another person.

This energy, even though it comes from one source, goes through changes as it flows downward. These changes reflect the conditions needed for its various functions. For instance, healing energy is a very pure form of this energy. It should be sent out in the same intensity as it had when received from the Higher Source. A good healer will have a pure channel through which to send the energy. If the healer's heart is not pure, the energy can change and lose its intensity.

Using heart energy to understand a problem is another function. Since this energy is kept within the person, it needs less intensity to achieve its purpose. The energy will have a calmer, more passive feeling. Because it is less intense, the reflection within can last a long time. This is what happens in meditation. The energy is soothing and calm and can sustain the person for long periods.

Heart energy is the force behind everything you do or believe in. This energy inspires you with creative ideas. It is the energy of love and compassion. Heart energy is you in your Higher Self and you in your everyday ego self. It contains all mundane, polarized thinking and experience, and also the wisdom of the ancients. It is an ever-expanding and ever-growing energy that expresses itself in many ways. For example, the energy of the heart will fill a person with warmth and kindness, and then change into an energy that aspires to greater knowledge.

Your heart contains both the higher energies and the energies coming from your emotions. The qualities of these energies are varied, but the container through which they flow is the same. Think of yourself as a living vessel full of energy. This energy is what makes you live, breathe and feel emotion. It is the energy of suffering, as well as the energy of love. Both flow through the heart center, and both impact the physical body.

The higher energy that comes from a universal source keeps your heart tuned. It regulates the amount of energy you need to have at a given time. The part that is not regulated comes from your personal emotions. Emotions will block the higher energy if they are negative. Positive emotions will be absorbed into the higher energy. Love will be enhanced by the Higher Source. Anger will block the natural flow from the source. Emotions, therefore, play an important part in working with your heart center. Often, they will cloud answers or change them according to personal needs.

It is impossible to see higher energy. It is totally invisible when it is inside you, but you can see energy in the air energy, that is part of nature, energy that is similar to your own energy, and that flows from the same source. If you go to the seashore and watch the water at sunset or in the early morning, you may see sparks floating through the air. These sparks are particles of energy that become visible when the energy of the water connects with the air. Energy like this is also flowing through your system. It is your life force, or what is often referred to as psychic energy.

Another type of energy comes from the Higher Self. When you begin to connect and communicate with the Higher Self, its energy transmits through the heart in a very gentle and loving way.

Lastly, the energy of the heart is the way to find your own inner spirit. To open your heart means to begin to attain spiritual wisdom and to learn about nature and its laws.

All of the above are ways that heart energy manifests. Yet, there still remains a whole area of the heart center that has energy not normally used— an area of mystery. In it are the intuition, the inner knowing, the seer, the priestess or priest, the meditator, the philosopher, and the mystical lover. This is your mythical self, the self of dreams, the self that holds your true essence.

This area of the heart is the true chalice. Its energy does not flow outward toward others, but instead flows further within, sometimes achieving magic or miracles. It answers your deepest wishes. This part of the heart, this energy, is the poet, the artist, and the dreamer. When you connect with it, you begin a journey into the unknown, a journey very few people begin. When the heart center begins to be activated, this part will become apparent.

In beginning your work with heart energy, it is best to take one kind of energy and experiment with it. In this way, you can determine for yourself the different qualities. The first and most recognizable energy is the energy of emotions. Take, for instance, the emotion of love. If you feel love toward someone, your heart will feel pressure, movement, expansion, or warmth.

Try the following exercise:

> *Pick someone you really think you love.*
> *Picture the person in your mind's eye, and then place*
> *the image into your heart center, asking: "What are my*
> *true feelings about ___?"*
> *Experience your heart's response.*
> *Keep visualizing the person and feeling what is in your*
> *heart.*

You should feel a strong response in your heart center. If you feel nothing or very little, it's possible you don't love the person as much as you think you do, or your heart is blocked. It's good to go back at another time and try the exercise again. If you're feeling irritated or out of sorts, this also can stop the reaction. Practice this exercise, but only with one person at a time; otherwise, there may be an overlap.

Whether the emotions are love or hate, they come from a deep source within. As feelings of love begin to emerge through the heart center, they take on an intensity of feeling. The love will either be very strong and passionate, or peaceful and calm. All are energies that the heart center processes. These energies are the conduits of your inner emotions and form what is referred to as the desire body. Any desire, whether positive or negative, resides in this part of you.

The desire body produces feelings and sends them through the center to materialize on the physical plane. For example, a college student has a desire to pass his exams. He will feel that desire very strongly in his heart. The energy of that desire can motivate the student to do well, or it can freeze into fear and inhibit the student, blocking his positive motivation and reversing its effect.

When the heart processes emotions, it does so in accordance with each individual's needs. Since individual needs vary so radically from person to person, there is no set determination on how much energy is processed or how strong or mild it is. The main thing to realize is that emotional energy is constant, and if the energy becomes negative, it can cloud the heart center so that none of the other energies can flow through it freely. For example, if you are angry and irritated about something, it is very difficult to be inspired or creative.

With the emotions comes a mechanism that regulates heart activity. If the emotions are too strong, the heart will literally turn itself off because it can't contain all the intensity. That's why a person will keep feeling the same emotions over and over again about a given situation. It's not that he can't drop it: it's because there is so much emotion in the unconscious that it can't all be processed at once. Sometimes the emotion will shut down completely and a person will think that he is over it, but then, a year, or even more, later, the same emotion will come up again.

The heart might be seen as a container varying in size from small to large. It can only hold a certain amount of energy, depending on its size. You enlarge the container by working with your heart on a regular basis.

Emotions take up a lot of the heart's activity. Alfred Lord Tennyson said, "It is better to have loved and lost than to never have loved at all." However, love can be good and/or bad, depending on how it is used. Here is a story that illustrates this:

> A young man fell in love with a beautiful woman
> who was an evil witch. He was totally under her spell.
> She kept demanding that he bring her things, and he

would willingly find anything her heart desired just to be with her.

One day, she beckoned to him and said she wanted the heart of his mother to eat for supper. Even though he loved his mother, he couldn't say no to the witch. He went home, killed his mother, and cut out her heart.

He ran as fast as he could back to the witch. Not looking, he suddenly fell across a stone in the road, and the heart went flying from his hand. As it landed next to him on the ground, it cried out, "Have you hurt yourself, my dear son?"

Inspiration and creativity are also energies processed by the heart center. These energies can be full of life and enthusiasm, or they can be quiet and calm. This energy can flow through you quickly, or it can be a slow energy that comes in what might be called glimpses of insights. The important thing to remember is that this energy comes through the heart. When you are feeling it, you can link with your heart and receive additional energy. The more you do this, the stronger it becomes.

Creative people have a direct connection to this source. Rarely do they lack inspiration. Everyone has the ability to achieve a high amount of inspiration. This aptitude comes from allowing the child to be expressive. When this is not encouraged, the aptitude is not developed. Working with the heart will bring that natural ability back.

Everyone has the ability to access the source of wisdom and knowledge. This usually comes through the heart from the Higher Self. This is part of your ability to grow in understanding. The energy of the Higher Self is very diverse. It will appear in a manner that is most appropriate for you at a given time in your life. For instance, someone's Higher Self may at one time appear to be a gentle wise man or woman. At another time it may be a warrior knight. This would be in keeping with specific information you need to learn at the time.

In working with the energies of your heart, you may find yourself unable to contain them all. There is a general fear that too much energy in the heart will be destructive. To keep the energy regulated is a matter of learning your own personal makeup. If you naturally have a lot of energy, you are someone who has to handle heart energy carefully; otherwise you could become fatigued. You need to notice when you go into harmful extremes. One reaction might be having palpitations in the heart center. It is best, then, to breathe slowly, link with your Higher Self, and try to become calmer. Naturally, if you are having palpitations in your physical heart, you should go to a doctor.

Someone who has a calm personality can handle heart energy better. This type of person can contain it and use it sparingly. Usually meditation is a key to having a calmer personality. Someone who meditates can handle heart energy very well.

What needs to be looked at and examined when you use your heart is not only how to use it, but when not to use it. Often a person feels it is important to love everyone, without taking into consideration whether the recipient of that love really wants it or is really helped by it. The following is a true story illustrating how using your heart to help others can be wrong:

> A friend's mother was a very wealthy woman living in England in the 1920s. The family owned a large estate and rented out land to the local farmers. When the mother died, the farmers came to the father and demanded money, claiming the mother had been giving them a monthly allowance. This allowance had been going on for years, unbeknownst to the father. Not only was he not able to continue this practice, but because of the depressed economy, he was also forced to sell his land.
>
> The farmers could no longer afford to rent from the new owner. Since they had developed no other skills, it was impossible for them to make a livelihood. The mother's compassionate gift ended up hurting them. If they had not received it, they would have tried to make the lands produce more and could have bought the land for themselves.

When you use your heart's energy, it is important to never force it on someone not ready to receive it, even when you feel it will benefit the person; to do so would be an infringement. Working with your heart center will help you determine whether the person really wants your help.

Each time you use your heart in a positive manner, a change in your perceptions occurs. It is a very slight change, but with time and constant use, you will begin to experience a sense of knowing that is very different from the mind's knowing.

For example, you may be speaking with someone you sense is upset. Your heart will tell you to say something that may make it easier for the person to talk about what's happening. As you listen, your heart will respond in a way that continues to be helpful. If you had used your mind instead, you might have asked the person, "What's wrong?" in a manner that is invasive. Using your mind to respond can come from a sense of "I can fix it," rather than a sense of what the person really needs.

Much of the work in learning to communicate is simply learning to listen with your heart and respond from an inner sense of understanding. When you come from a place of knowing within, you will always feel it in your heart. The truth of the knowledge resides there.

With each relationship, there are always hidden factors. Not only do we have past and present conditioning, but we also carry within us needy emotions and desires that we hope will be fulfilled in the relationship. These desires can block seeing and hearing clearly. Many misunderstandings are caused by this and are perpetuated as a person goes from relationship to relationship.

To determine whether you are reacting to someone from your heart or from an inner personal desire or need is difficult. Usually, a way of checking is to place the name or an image of the individual into your heart and ask the Higher Self for more understanding. However, if your neediness or desire is strong enough, it can cloud the Higher Self. It's good to be aware of such strong personal desires, for then you know you have to be very clear in the relationship, particularly if it is a romantic relationship where all one's needs can be awakened and looking at the relationship objectively can become impossible. The best thing to do in a case like that is to stay calm and detached. Let go of as much emotion as possible, and then try the exercise of asking for better understanding.

Everyone has a sense of discrimination within—an unconscious knowing about something or someone. Determining whether a relationship would be a good one comes from this inner knowing. Using discrimination in relationships would save many broken hearts. This part in you can really feel the positive and negative qualities of a person and determine how those qualities would interact with yours.

Using discrimination can be helpful not only in personal relationships but in your work as well. Discrimination can help you to know the right approach and way to conduct a specific business project.

Discrimination is not intuition. They differ in their ability to determine right from wrong. Discrimination is based on knowledge, whereas intuition comes from the senses. Here's an example: You are interviewing an applicant for work. Your intuition senses there is something 'off' about the person. Your discrimination would advise you to ask more questions than usual to determine if the person knows the work. Having one without the other can be unbalanced. Discrimination without intuition can be cold and calculating. Intuition without discrimination can be too ungrounded. Both working together are very powerful.

With each use of your heart, there is a way to check whether you are working with discrimination and intuition or with emotion. Emotion can cloud them both. You can practice with the following exercise:

Exercise:

> *Go through the process of connecting with your heart center.*
> *When you feel connected, place an image of someone or something you need to understand better in your heart and experience the energy that comes up in you.*
> *If the energy feels balanced, ask to be given more understanding.*
> *If the energy feels strong and emotional, let it slowly die down...then, once again, place the object or person into your heart and this time ask your Higher Self to help you clarify the problem. If the energy comes up again in the same way, you know there is too much emotion around this subject for you to get a clear indication.*
> *If this is the case, ask your Higher Self to send you understanding in another manner.*

You may receive an answer at another time when you least expect it. It's sometimes easier for the Higher Self to get through to you when there is no time for emotions to arise and cloud it.

As you work with your heart energy, you will find that you begin to experience it differently from when you first started working with it. The energy itself will feel more refined, and there will be a definite quality to it that you can better identify. Remember, all of these practices take time and commitment.

4

Accessing and Using Heart Energy

Heart energy is a specific type of energy coming from the Source, or what can also be called the God Consciousness. This energy comes down to the heart in a much lesser form. Since the Source's energy is the highest, no human could receive it directly in its pure form. The intensity would be destructive. Therefore, the energy is modified so that a human heart can hold it.

When we refer here to the human heart, we refer to the heart center, not the physical heart. The heart energy is usually warm in feeling. An example would be the warm feeling you have toward a loved one. The energy will expand in the center and move outward toward the person for whom you are feeling love. This love energy varies according to how much love you have for the person.

Personal love uses this energy, but there is another kind of love that experiences the energy differently. This love is what is called impersonal or disidentified love. I prefer calling it disidentified love rather than impersonal love. The word impersonal has some negative connotations attached to it, such as not caring. Disidentified love means not attached, yet carrying with it pure love feelings. This disidentified love is far stronger than personal love. It is a love that encompasses all humans and experiences all their feelings because it is not attached to the self.

This heart energy is what is used when someone feels compassion in its purest sense. To access this energy and use it is something that everyone needs to learn. Unfortunately, most people cannot do this, as they need to have achieved a higher state of spirituality to do so. Yet, even at a beginning stage, you can certainly learn some of the methods of accessing this energy.

Let's do an exercise that will introduce this energy to you.

Exercise:

If you haven't yet chosen a Higher Self exercise to work with, do that now. They are at the back of this book entitled "Working With the Higher Self." When you feel you are linked to the Higher Self, ask it the following questions:

> *Is it possible for me to experience, even for a moment, the feeling of pure heart energy?*
> *If the answer is yes, ask the Higher Self to let you experience it.*
> *If the answer is no, ask: Why can't I experience it at this time?*
> *What do I need to do to experience this energy more?*
> *Do I have any blocks to working with this energy?*
> *How can I distinguish when I am using personal love energy and when I am using the disidentified love energy?*
> *Is there a practice I can do to help me open up the disidentified love energy more?*
> *If you receive a practice, take time now to follow the practice and experience how it feels for you. If you don't receive a practice, ask the Higher Self why, and also ask what needs to happen for you to receive one.*

Sometimes a person isn't ready because of other things she is working on. The timing needs to be correct in order to experience the best approach for learning how to access the heart energy. Don't feel discouraged if you are not ready at this time. Instead, ask the Higher Self to give you a simple exercise for using your heart that you can work with in the meantime.

The above exercise will introduce you to the impersonal love energy and how it feels. There is a lot more that needs to be done in order to begin using it more consciously. I suggest that you stay with the exercise above and work on the answers from the Higher Self for at least two to three weeks, or until you feel ready to go on to the next exercise. When you believe you are ready, check with the Higher Self to see if you can continue to the second exercise.

This chapter will take you a few weeks to complete. It is important not to rush through the chapter. Each step needs to be taken slowly. The personal practice you are given in the first exercise should also be done slowly. Don't change the practice when you go on to the next exercise; only change it if your Higher Self gives you another practice to do.

The following is a true story that took place many years ago.

A woman was studying a yoga teaching in the south of India. Her teacher was a well-known guru who usually only worked with men, but because this woman had been with him many times in past lives, he decided to accept her as his student.

Her name was Marianne and she was from England. Since she was the only woman student, when she came to the ashram she lived in separate quarters by herself. She attended classes and had private sessions with her teacher. She was doing very well in her practice until a new student arrived at the ashram.

This student was an Englishman named John, who became a devotee and, later, a disciple. When Marianne met her fellow countryman, she fell madly in love with him. Obviously, they had been together in a past life, as he also was attracted to her. Both were in a teaching that was celibate, and both decided to stay away from each other so there would be little temptation. This continued for one year, but both felt such love in their hearts for each other that finally, one night, John went to Marianne's dwelling and they made love.

Soon their lovemaking could not be stopped. Their passion for each other was overwhelming. Their teacher, of course, realized what was happening but didn't say anything to them. He was waiting for them to come to him.

Finally, they confessed to him with great shame, knowing they would be expelled from the ashram. He told them, "You have great love for each other from having been together many times in many ways. This love you feel is personal love and needs to be played out. Leave the ashram and live together until your passion has been fulfilled, then come back to me and learn how to change your personal love to disidentified love; in so doing you will open your hearts to divine love and use that divine love to help others. Personal love is the first step in doing that."

"How can that be the first step?" Marianne asked.

"Because personal love energy opens the heart, making it a bigger container for the Source's energy. It leads the way, and that is why it often is the first step."

They followed their teacher's advice and left the ashram, returning to England where they lived together and went back to the work they'd been doing before they went to the ashram. They even married and had a child, a son. When their son left home to go to college, they returned to the ashram and resumed their yoga practice. In a few years they achieved the higher initiations and eventually became teachers themselves. Both learned to work with the disidentified love of the heart center, and in so doing, were able to drop their personal love for one another and change it to disidentified love, which they could feel not only with each other but also with everyone they encountered. Eventually, when their teacher died, they returned to England and taught there.

When you have personal love, it can help you expand your center and make it ready to contain the higher energy. Sometimes people lose that desire when they become too immersed in personal love. It's best to go through that, but not to forget the goal. Disidentified love refines who you are and takes you to a place where you can handle the higher energies, whereas personal love stays in your desire body, and the desire body can most definitely stop your spiritual growth if you give in to it too much. That's why it is important to do everything in moderation.

Exercise:

> *It is important to think through this exercise before trying to do it. Therefore, read through the exercise, think about each step, and maybe add what works better for you. If you feel there should be another step, try including it. Sometimes an exercise needs to be expanded,*

or even the opposite, made smaller. Decide that before even attempting to do it.

When you are ready, ask yourself the following questions:

When I concentrate on my heart center, how do I experience it? List everything you feel and even list everything you think.

How do I determine if the energy is coming from above or is simply my own life energy?

Are there some people I feel more heart energy toward? If this is true, do I understand why?

When I send heart energy to others, how does that make my heart feel?

When I love someone and feel irritated with them, how does that change the energy?

Is there anyone I genuinely feel disidentified love for?

Can I truly tell the difference between personal and disidentified love? Describe the difference in detail.

What happens when I feel personal love being directed toward me?

What happens when I feel disidentified love energy coming toward me?

Can I receive personal love and in turn send back disidentified love?

What happens when someone sends me disidentified love? How can I tell it is disidentified? Describe the difference.

When I am alone, can I think about someone and feel love for that person, or do I physically have to be with them?

How can I change personal love to disidentified love?

What is my next best step to learning disidentified love?

If you find it difficult to answer some of these questions yourself, ask your Higher Self to help you.

We have been describing love energy that comes through the heart. That is just one kind of heart energy. There are several other kinds of energy that use the heart as their vehicle. The following is a list of the different types:

- Love energy
- Wisdom energy
- Healing energy
- Creative energy
- Motivational energy
- Discrimination energy
- Divine energy

1. **Love energy** is the most common, and the one which most people feel is the only energy coming through the heart center. However, this is just one specific energy. There are six more types of energy that come through the heart center.

2. **Wisdom energy** flows from very high sources. It comes from the higher mind, which is part of your Higher Self, into the heart, and then it can flow back to the higher mind. Wisdom energy has access to higher knowledge and can bring that knowledge down into the consciousness by using both vehicles, higher mind and heart. It cannot come through just one vehicle. It needs both to fully function. Here is an example: The higher mind is striving to understand the meaning of God Consciousness. A concept can come through to the mind, resulting in a thought. When the thought is then put into the heart, more understanding comes and that, in turn, can return to the mind as a thought. This process can continue back and forth to find deeper and deeper understanding. If, instead, the concept only comes into the mind, it can get lost or not be understood correctly.

To illustrate further: If you ask the question, "What is the meaning of God Consciousness?" a thought may come into the mind, "It is the source of all life in the universe." If you take that thought and put it into the heart, you may come up with an 'aha' feeling that, "The source is pure energy." Taking that feeling back to the mind as a thought, the next thought in the mind could then be, "If it is pure energy, is it possible for me to experience it?" Taking that into your heart, you may begin to feel some energy warming your chest. Just let yourself feel the energy and become one with it, knowing in your mind that this was a gift from a Higher Source.

You can have access to wisdom at any time. The initial wisdom comes from the Higher Self, but it is your striving that deepens the experience and gives you more understanding.

Exercise:

> *Think of a question to which you would like to have an answer from higher wisdom.*
> *Go through the process of connecting with your heart center.*
> *Put the question in your heart, and when you receive an answer, put it into your mind. Then take whatever thought comes up and put that into your heart. Continue back and forth until you feel you have a deeper understanding of the answer to the original question.*

Wisdom energy can also come through at different times. If you are meditating on something and can't get an answer, the answer may come to you later, even in a dream. Be patient about receiving answers. Sometimes you can absorb something better when you are resting or are in a different location. For example, if you are in a room that is messy and has negative vibrations, it will be much more difficult for the answer to come through.

Out in nature is always a good place to receive, as the atmosphere is purer, with less human vibrations in it. Also, in a sacred place, like a church or synagogue, there is a better chance of receiving something, mainly because prayers have been recited repeatedly there, building strong, positive vibrations. If you receive something in a place outside your home, be certain to write it down and return to the above exercise later.

Exercise:

> *The ability to link with the higher wisdom is a very special ability that needs to be learned. Try asking a question once a week, but if you don't receive an answer in that week, continue asking the same question the following week. Don't ask another question until you have received an answer to the first question.*

One last thing to remember: Be certain to always write down your questions and the answers that come through. When you reread them at a later time, you may want to continue the process and learn more.

3. **Healing energy** is very different from any of the others. It is always sent from a Higher Source to a physical healer, who, in turn, sends it to the person who needs healing.

The energy is circular when it comes down. This is because the energy is extremely strong, and a circular motion reduces some of the intensity. Otherwise it would be too powerful for the healer to contain. Occasionally the energy can be direct because the receiver's spiritual nature is strong enough to receive it directly. This energy generally is warm, but in the case of a very bad disease, such as cancer, the energy comes from a Higher Source and is ice cold. The physical healer cannot pass it through for a lengthy period of time because of its power and cold feeling.

People who are natural healers usually have done this work before in a previous lifetime. Once one has been a healer, she continues to carry that characteristic with her from lifetime to lifetime. Sometimes a person can learn to become a healer at a later time, but usually that person has to have a good heart capable of holding the energy.

When a healer is working physically on a person, healing energy always comes through the heart and goes out through the hands. If the healing energy is instead sent directly to the sick person, that energy is sent directly from the heart to wherever the illness is. Usually, this energy penetrates the person's aura and goes directly to the affected area in the body. Distant sending, as it is called, works best with people who have some fear around hands-on healing. Hands-on healing works best with those who feel open to it coming in. A healer can feel the resistance from a patient when doing hands-on healing, and if that resistance is strong, it's best not to continue but to plan to send distant healing instead. Naturally, if the healer is not physically near the patient, there can only be distant healing.

Healing energy is a gift. Usually, when someone hears about a healer and goes to her, it is because the person is meant to receive this energy. Healing energy will change a person's consciousness, opening it up more to the spiritual.

If someone is meant to die, then the healing energy will also help that happen more quickly, so the person will have less suffering or pain.

4. **Creative energy** is full of a vibration that stimulates people's senses and thinking. It is a strong force that conveys ideas and heightens awareness to all possibilities. To access this energy you need to be in your heart, connect to the higher realms, ask for help and guidance, and send thoughts out into space of what you want to create. For example, if you aspire to paint a painting, you can ask to see a design that you can paint. If you are writing a story, you can link with the creative force and ask to be sent beautiful words that would make a wonderful story. The same is true if you are an inventor, or even a lawyer who has to defend a client.

Sometimes the energy is so strong that the person receiving it can't sit still but has to move around. Sometimes it's the opposite; the creative flow is calm and subtle. It still vibrates, but not as much. It's much subtler and more refined. This type of creativity needs to be nurtured and recognized; otherwise, it can go unnoticed.

Exercise:

> *In the morning, ask to receive creative energy for the work you will be doing. Then, at night, think back on the day and notice when that energy was sent to you. Did you recognize it? Did you utilize it? The more you use it, the more you will be sent. Also, recognize that it is from an outside source, and feel grateful for receiving it. Unfortunately, many creative people tap into this energy and think it is their own, which builds up the ego.*

5. **Motivational energy** is something that is unique in the human condition. What is it, you may ask? One example: When you need to accomplish a task you really don't want to do, you need to reach up and bring into your being a feeling, such as determination, which is a quality of the will, to help you do the task without procrastination. Even if the task is one that you really want to do, sometimes that energy has to be kindled in order to accomplish it. Reviewing why the task is important to do, and re-choosing it, can be helpful. The energy comes directly from your will.

Will energy, used correctly, motivates a person to carry through with a project and finish it. It also helps someone to look at all the possibilities that a project may have, in order to begin and finish it. It is an energy that needs to be learned through good, practical skills. Sometimes a person knows how to complete a project, but simply gets stuck and can't move forward. That's when she needs to focus on the will and strengthen it in order to overcome whatever is blocking the project.

It is important to determine how strong of a will you have and whether or not your will can accomplish a task at hand.

Exercise:

> *Look back at some of the projects you have accomplished and determine if you did them using motivational energy, employing the will within.*

Also, look at the projects you have not completed, and determine what was lacking. How was your will in this project? Did you try to use motivational energy at all? Can you go back now and complete something by using this energy?

In the future when you take on a project, I would suggest linking with your heart and your will and asking to use the motivational energy within you.

6. **Discrimination energy** comes from lifetimes of building it into your consciousness. You may wonder how that is done. Basically, as you evolve, you learn lessons that remain in your heart. These lessons build discrimination. For example, in this or a past lifetime you were punished for something you did that was illegal. Because of this punishment, you learned that doing illegal things could damage you. When confronted with a possible illegal action now, your discrimination knows it's best not to do it – you could be caught and jailed. The behavior may have to be repeated several times for the lesson to be learned. Perhaps you did not get caught every time you did the illegal action, and so you repeated such actions, again and again, until you learned that you would be caught.

When you meet a new person, if you have good discrimination concerning people, you can 'read' the person and know about her character. This comes from lifetimes of having to deal with different types of people. When you have no discrimination, you can be hurt over and over again because you lack the understanding of the true character of someone.

Through those experiences you learn who to trust and who not to trust, and thus build discrimination, which protects you when you encounter people with hidden negative motives.

Exercise:

Look back at some of your relationships in this life. Reflect on the ones that caused you harm or hurt, and notice whether early on you felt at all uneasy about the person involved. That uneasiness would be your discrimination telling you to be careful.

Sometimes strong attractions come from conditioning or past lives, and these attractions can be positive or negative. It's best to place the name or image of the person in your heart and ask yourself if this attraction is one that will prove positive or could prove negative.

*Your heart knows the answer. The more you listen to it,
the more you build discrimination.*

7. **Divine energy** is what your heart longs to receive. It is divine because it comes from the Source. This Source has many names in different cultures. Rather than calling it any of those names, such as God, I prefer to call it the Source so that it encompasses different cultures. This energy is full of bliss or what is sometimes called rapture. It fills the heart and overflows into the entire body, like a vessel overflowing into a stream. When a person feels this energy, even for a second, the experience cannot be put into words. Its feeling is too profound, and it leaves the person feeling an oneness with the Source. I like to think of it as a blessing given to humankind to help people strive to become one with it again. It inspires hope in eternity and the desire to change and grow spiritually.

Exercise:

*Link with your heart, then send your heart energy
upward toward the Source and ask to feel the divine
energy from it. Keep doing this exercise and you may
suddenly experience the divine energy.*

In this chapter, the energies of the heart were described. Each of these energies will be gone into more fully in separate chapters so that you can come to a better understanding of what they are, how they feel, and how you can begin to utilize them to help yourself and to benefit others. Heart energy is the key to real self-awareness and to learning compassion.

Opening the heart to allow these energies to flow in is a difficult task, mainly because the ego nature tries to prohibit you from using your heart in this way. The ego, the lower nature, and what is called the desire body keep people from feeling the heart. Instead, the ego works on fulfilling desires and on isolating a person from her true nature. The true nature resides in the heart center—not in the physical heart, which simply makes the body function, but in the heart chalice that contains all the above energies.

Once you begin to use your heart energies, you begin the process of opening your heart chalice, and during this process, you will experience a change in yourself. Part of that change involves a new awareness of who you are, both in the positive and in the negative. Then comes the awareness of who you can become. With that awareness, you will slowly start to change your consciousness. Your negative characteristics can then be acknowledged, understood, and transmuted if you have a deep desire to do so. Once you begin using your heart energy, it opens you to a longing for more spiritual knowledge and understanding.

When the heart opens, it is like a lotus blossom that blooms upon the water, but under the water are the roots embedded in the dirt. Those roots, and the dirt, will also be awakened. This represents the battle of a person's lower nature with their higher nature. This is what is called the spiritual journey.

In the process of this journey, many things will happen. Some things will prove joyful and others will be barriers that have to be overcome. Having access to the heart's energy is a means to confront those barriers and pass over or through them, knowing that they are simply barriers and they can never stop your journey.

As you work with these energies, you will experience resistance and sometimes feel the way is too difficult. Remember to link with your heart during those times, feel its warmth, and know that nothing is too difficult.

5

The Heart's True Functions

The heart chalice has many functions. Some of these were mentioned in the last chapter on the different types of energy that pass through the heart. Besides energy, the heart also contains knowledge that is part of a person's individuality. The individuality is comprised of all the positive and negative characteristics that have been played out and accumulated through many lifetimes. If you don't believe in past lives, you can call these accumulations part of the collective unconscious, a term coming from the research of Carl Jung, a famous psychotherapist in the last century.

These accumulations carry aspects of the different cultures on the planet, and those aspects in turn constitute hidden qualities that can emerge during your lifetime.

If your heart is functioning with the positive qualities, then you will appear to others as a warm-hearted, kind, and loving person. If your heart is functioning with the negative qualities, you will appear to others as cold, distant and uncaring. Sometimes a person will operate with both qualities. Depending on a person's mood, he may appear loving or cold.

Since everyone's personality can contain both positive and negative characteristics, it would be helpful to identify what these are for you.

Exercise:

> *Think about how you feel toward certain people. Make*
> *a list of your associates, people you know, and also your*

family, friends and fellow workers. After you have made
the list, take each name, place it in your heart center,
and ask yourself how you feel about this person.
If you have a warm feeling, note that next to the name.
Then ask yourself: Why do I feel warmth toward this
person?
If you have a cold feeling, mark that next to the name.
Then ask yourself: Why do I feel coldness toward this
person?
In doing this exercise, you can begin to determine how
you use your heart constantly to express your inner feel-
ings.
Look at the list of those for whom you feel coldness, and
taking one name at a time, ask yourself the following
questions:
Is it possible for me to change my feelings toward this
person?
If the answer is yes, ask: What is the best way to do this?
If the answer is no, ask: Is there anything about this
person that I can feel warm about?

It's possible that each person towards whom you feel coldness has an aspect in his personality that you dislike. If you can find something positive in the person, you may be able to change the feeling of dislike to neutral. The person may never be a close friend, but maybe you can begin to feel some warmth toward him because of the positive trait. It's a good practice to do this in order to change a cold heart to one that is always functioning as a warm heart.

Some people come into this life having a warm heart naturally. Such a person could also have developed this type of heart because he had warm-hearted parents, especially a warm-hearted mother. Such childhood conditioning helps build a positively functioning heart.

Exercise:

Ask yourself the following questions:
What kind of heart quality does my mother have?
What kind of heart quality does my father have?
If you have siblings, consider each one and ask what
kind of heart quality the sibling has.

> *If you have close relatives, reflect on each name and ask what kind of heart quality each one has.*
> *Try to remember your teachers in school, and considering each name, ask what kind of heart quality the teacher had.*
> *Take the names of all your close friends and ask what kind of heart quality each of them has.*

When you do this exercise, divide your responses into two sections, placing the warm-hearted people on one side and the cold-hearted ones on the other. If some of the people have a combination heart quality of warm and cold, list these separately.

Sometimes a person is attracted to someone with the opposite quality. If you are warm-hearted, someone who seems cold and distant may intrigue you. That person may be an intellectual who interests you. And the opposite is true: if you are cold and distant, you may be attracted to someone who is warm and caring. You may be a bit afraid of such a person, but the warmth will draw you in.

When the heart is working with warmth, it can hold qualities that are rare and difficult to obtain: for example, compassion, deeper understanding, the ability to mirror someone, helping someone remain centered, sending calming energy to someone who is feeling emotional, and also the ability to comfort and send caring feelings to someone who is having difficulties.

These types of heart functions make a difference in any relationship. When you truly use your heart to connect to someone, you can experience what the person is feeling, and only then can you help him. Otherwise, you are in your own feelings of what the person needs from you, and those feelings may be incorrect.

Exercise:

> *Try an experiment. Ask a good friend to do it with you. Sit opposite each other. Each one of you thinks of a difficult situation that you are or were in that the friend doesn't know. Talk superficially about it, but don't say what you really are feeling or need to say. Make it surface talk. Each of you also link with your heart and try to link to the other person's heart. Try to understand intuitively the hidden things that are not being said,*

*and then try to respond from your intuitive sense, in a
kind and loving way.*

You will be surprised at some of the insights you begin to have, insights that can really be helpful. Every time you meet with someone, do this exercise silently inside and try to listen with your heart. The more you practice this, the less difficult it becomes. It's a way of developing the true functions of your heart.

Using your intuition is another function of your heart. The intuition is an energy that is felt in the heart and is in both men and women. It is thought to be exclusive to women, however there are many men who have developed it just as much. They call this ability an instinct or a gut feeling.

Intuition feels or senses whether something could happen or whether someone is doing the right thing. It is based on positive instincts and when listened to, is always correct. The problem is that many people do not follow their intuition. Haven't you heard someone say, "I felt that would happen, but I didn't believe my feelings?" This is because the intuition is nebulous and sometimes abstract, often it is only remembered after something has happened.

Generally, the intuition is given to a person from the Higher Self that understands right action. If you are very intuitive but doubt your intuition, a good way of checking it is to link with your Higher Self and ask it if what you are feeling is correct.

Exercise:

*Link with your Higher Self, and then ask it the following
questions:*
Is my intuition developed?
If the answer is no, ask: What is a process to start developing it?
*If the answer is yes, ask: Do I listen to it most of the
time?*
If the answer is no, ask: Why not? Then ask for a process that will help you to start listening to it.

When you have an intuitional sense or feeling, always write it down in a notebook so you can check it out. Was it correct? Or was it not the intuition but something else, such as a feeling coming from your desires?

Sometimes intuition comes very quickly. It's there, just for a second, and almost instantly you forget it. If this is the case for you, ask your Higher Self to help you remember and also to help you realize when you have an intuitional feeling.

Intuition can make a difference in all your relationships. In the previous exercise of mirroring someone, if you used your intuition then you had a much better understanding of the person. Whenever you try to mirror someone, add the thought, "May I also use my intuition when I am doing this mirroring."

If you don't feel your intuition is developed, then it's best to proceed slowly. Always take the time to try to feel something about a situation before you use your mind to figure it out. Intuitive people who are mentally oriented will often not use their intuition, but instead rely on their mind. Even if you have a good mind, the intuition, which comes from a Higher Source, is always more correct. A valuable practice is to write down what you feel and also what you think is the right action. When they differ, pick one and see whether it or the other turns out to be correct.

Another important function of the heart is the ability to feel how another person feels, but often one cannot necessarily feel how another person is truly feeling. Although that ability is part of a refined sense of compassion, it differs from compassion because it is simply feeling the other's emotions; it does not include sending compassionate energy to the other person. Rather, it is a more sympathetic kind of sensitivity.

Only a select few people can be so sensitive as to totally pick up what someone else is feeling. Usually that's not a good thing to do, as you can literally take on emotions that are not your own. If you are such a sensitive person, it's wise to protect yourself. I suggest first sensing if the person you are talking with is carrying a heavy burden, and if you start to feel this, immediately imagine placing a glass bell around your whole body. This step protects you from taking on any burdensome feelings, and you can still help the person by using your intuition and heart to pick up information. You can then say that you are feeling such and such from the person, and determine if you can be of help. The ability to be sensitive often has to be worked with carefully in order to develop it into a positive function rather than an overwhelming one. If you are not overly sensitive, you can immediately be in touch with what is happening without taking the feelings on, and then address it by stating what you are sensing and asking if you can be of help.

Sometimes a person is not overly sensitive but has the ability to be in certain situations, for example, in close relationships with people seen on a regular basis. A person can usually pick up the feelings toward himself from his loved one rather easily. Becoming more sensitive in this manner is very positive.

Exercise:

> *Ask yourself: Am I sensitive to the feelings of others? If so, how does picking up feelings affect me?*
> *If you feel you are over sensitive, ask: How can I protect myself more from taking the feelings on?*
> *If you are not someone who is generally sensitive and sympathetic, ask: Am I able to pick up what my loved ones are feeling?*
> *If you feel you cannot do this, link with your heart and ask: How can I become more sensitive to the feelings of my loved ones? Also, ask for a first step in this process.*

Developing this ability in moderation is helpful not only with loved ones but also when you are working with others closely. If someone is having a problem with you, which he is unable to express, you can then address it yourself by saying, "I'm feeling a certain type of energy from you. Can you tell me what the problem is?"

If the person says there isn't a problem between you, then ask if the person has another issue that is bothering him. It's important to clear out hidden emotions, for when they are buried, they will affect the relationship. This is true about any group you are in, whether it is family, friends, work, or associations. Addressing feelings is always important, but remember, in any confrontation, you need to stay centered in your heart.

Another function of your heart is the way in which you send love energy. You may feel that there isn't a particular method to do this and that it is automatic – you love someone and it just comes out naturally. Generally this is true, but there are situations in which it is best not to send love, and other situations in which you can literally send love.

The situation when it is best not to feel loving or to send love, naturally, is when the person you love is focused on work and does not need to be disturbed in any way. Sending love at this time would be an interruption. Even if the person doesn't realize what is happening, there will be a distraction. And if you physically approach the person and are affectionate, that also is not good timing.

A situation for purposefully sending love is when you see or feel your loved one is upset or in conflict. You can send him love and specify that the love be used to eliminate some of his feelings. For example, your child is having a difficult test at school. Sending him love can help lessen his anxiety. Or, another example, a friend of yours is interviewing for a job. Again, sending love can help relieve some of the anxiety he is feeling in the interview.

How to handle the above two situations is very individual. In the first case, when the person is focused on work, not to feel loving simply means containing your love. You can send thoughts of encouragement for the project, or simply try not to think about what your loved one is doing by running an errand or focusing on some work of your own.

Sending love intentionally means linking with your Higher Self and asking it to send love through the other person's Higher Self. This is the best way to do this, as the other person's Higher Self then regulates it. You don't want to send too much, as it might disturb the person; nor do you want to send too little, as it won't take away the feelings you want to help eliminate.

Exercise:

> *Write down the names of the people you have genuine love feelings for. Taking each name, ask yourself the following questions:*
> *Am I aware of when I should not send love to this person? If the answer is no, ask your Higher Self: What would be a good indicator for me to watch for?*
> *Then, taking the same name, ask: Am I aware of when I need to directly send love to this person? If the answer is no, ask your Higher Self: How can I become aware of when I need to send love directly to this person?*

Another function of the heart is using the heart energy to comfort someone. This is not the same as sending love to someone. Comfort is a whole different type of energy. You may be in a situation where someone needs comforting and you don't even know the person. Good examples are when you encounter a child who is lost, or an elderly senile person who doesn't know where he is, or someone you only met once who needs help. You may also come upon an accident where someone is hurt and needs comforting until a doctor arrives. Those are some situations with strangers, but often friends and family need comfort when they are in situations that are upsetting for them.

Comforting is also considered a feminine quality. Yet, there are many men who have this ability naturally. We think of women who nurture and comfort their children when they are sick, yet there are also many men who do the same for their children. Everyone needs to develop this ability, but of all the functions of the heart, this one is used least. If you came from a family that was not nurturing, then you would not know how to simply comfort someone. You can have a warm heart quality, and even send love, but not know what a person needs at a time of upset. Comfort is being there, listening, even doing physical things like getting the person something to eat or drink, or simply holding the person if he is crying. The latter is often difficult for someone to do, even when the person loves him, and it can even be more difficult if you encounter a crying person you don't know. It's easier to hold a child who is crying than an adult. Comforting is a function of the heart that often needs to be developed.

Exercise:

> *Ask yourself the following questions:*
> *Do I try to comfort someone who I can tell is upset or in some distress?*
> *If the answer is no, go through the process of connecting with your heart center, then ask: How can I best learn to do this?*
> *If I do try to comfort someone who needs comforting, do I feel comfortable in doing it? If the answer is no, connect with your heart and ask: How can I begin to feel more natural in doing this?*

Think about your childhood. Did your parents comfort you when you needed it? How about your relatives, your grandparents? Did any of them comfort you when you needed it? If you experience discomfort in comforting someone, examine your background more closely to find where that could be coming from. Try to notice if someone needs comforting, and even though it's difficult for you, try doing it, especially if it's a loved one.

Sometimes a person's cultural background is an indicator about being able to comfort. The Latin races are more affectionate and demonstrative, and would have an easier time than those from the northern countries, such as England, Germany, and Holland, etc. Look at your background and determine if culture is also a factor.

Learning how to comfort someone is developing a very important and positive function of the heart. Doing this opens a person's heart and develops other aspects of it, ones that constitute genuine warmth. If you are more mentally oriented, learning how to comfort with your heart will bring you more into balance.

One precaution: Do not comfort someone who does not want to be comforted. If a person is crying, he does not necessarily want to be touched and held. Always ask the person if you can put your arm around him. To be overly comforting can be annoying to someone who may just want to be alone. The best thing to do is ask: "Can I get you something? Can I help in any way?" It's important to honor a person's needs. This is true for a loved one and for a stranger. Never force comfort onto anyone, but be there for him if he needs it.

The last function of the heart is the ability to hold a loved one within. This literally means keeping that person in the heart in a contained manner and not communicating your feelings for him. The reasons for containing your love include: if you love him too much, you feel a lot of sympathy for what he is going through, or you have a desire for him to achieve a lot. These kinds of feelings should not be expressed to the person, yet you still feel them and can't let them go. For example, you have a deep need for your child to do really well in school. Expressing that need can disturb your child and make him feel your strong expectations. Instead, keep those expectations in your heart, hidden from him. It's a difficult task for most people, and needs to be learned.

The learning process here means you have to completely disidentify from the feelings you have. Acknowledge the feelings, consciously put them into your heart, ask for help from your Higher Self to contain them in your heart, and never express them or send those feelings to the person. If the feelings are contained, they will not affect him. If you can't contain them, then even unconsciously the person will feel the emotional energy coming from you.

Parents have many expectations of their children, which often prevent the children from doing as well as they could. Having expectations and other feelings is also true within a marriage, or an intimate relationship, and even between close friends. It's always best to let such feelings go completely, but there are times someone can't do that.

Exercise:

> *Take the list of names of the people you are close to, and for each one, put the name in your heart and ask the following questions:*

*Do I have any feelings toward this person that I need to
let go?*
*If the answer is yes, ask: What is my main feeling? Then
ask: Can I let it go?*
*If the answer is no, then connect with your Higher Self
and ask: Please help me to contain this feeling in my
heart and not let the person receive it.*

If the feeling is a strong one, you may experience it coming up over and over with pressure to express it. Each time, link again with your Higher Self and ask for help to contain the feeling in your heart.

If you find you can't contain it well enough, you can try telling the person what you are feeling, explaining that it is your feeling and you just need to discuss it with him. Then let the conversation continue, but remember, your feeling can be based on truth or on a misjudgment. The main thing is to be disidentified so you can sense whether the responses are true.

The only exception to this process is when you see a loved one doing something that is dangerous to his well being and health. Then it is important to express your concern.

In general, the heart function is a very strong indicator of a person's individuality. Being warm hearted is a quality that most people want to develop. Doing the exercises in this chapter and this book will lead you in that direction.

6

When the Heart Fails to Function

When I say the heart fails to function, I am not referring to the death process but another kind of death. It is the death of positive emotions. There are many reasons for this to happen. One of the main situations is a loss of a loved one, whether it is in a break-up or literally, when the person dies. Heartbreak of any kind stops the heart from functioning, and it can take a long time for the heart to regain what it had previously.

Sometimes when the loss is too much, the heart remains stilled and never comes back to its normal functioning. This chapter is for those of you who have had that happen and also for those of you who know someone who is in this condition.

Unfortunately, it becomes almost impossible to help someone who is going through this. You can comfort the person and be there for the person, but permanent loss puts a wound in the heart that most often takes a long time to heal. Some people have the strength to go forward and heal the heart quickly, whereas others can get stuck in the wound.

First, let's consider the person who knows someone like this. What is the best way to use your heart to help the wounded one recover? First, with comfort. Second, by using your intuition to know what to say and what kind of help to give, and third, by simply being there for the person to lean on, to cry to, and to confide in. But there is one more thing you can do.

Usually when someone is wounded with loss, she goes into an inner child that feels lost, especially if the person has a wounded inner child. Because this happens, the person then feels doubly wounded and lost herself. It's important to help that person regain the mature self and not remain in the inner child. If she cannot move out of her inner child, then explain to her that she may need to do therapy on her inner child, not just grief therapy. This may be difficult for the person to accept, but it's important for you to say anyway. Do so gently and with love.

If you are the person who has suffered the loss, then check with your Higher Self and ask if you have a wounded child within that is suffering even more pain and confusion now that this current loss happened. If the answer is yes, then my advice is to seek help from a therapist.

There are other situations that can cause the loss of positive heart emotions. I want to go into these more fully, as in all cases the feelings of loss can be eased and stopped. Other reasons for feeling deep loss include the following:

1. Feeling too much pressure to complete a project and giving up.

2. Feeling that something that you want will never happen for you, and the disappointment is extreme.

3. Loss of hope around feelings of love toward someone who does not reciprocate. This is different from having been with someone for a long time and having broken up with that person.

4. Knowing that your goals in life can never be fulfilled because of several mundane factors.

5. Seeing others succeed and feeling discouraged about yourself.

6. Wanting more than you can have.

7. Looking at life through dark glasses, as a glass half empty.

8. Having a huge inner critic that makes you feel unworthy.

9. Seeing yourself in a negative manner.

10. Looking at the future with no enthusiasm.

All of the above are negative points of view that overwhelm positive ones to the point that the positive energies of the heart can no longer function. Each of them stems from childhood conditioning, or from tendencies that you bring over from past lives, or from the collective unconscious influences. They can come from all these causes. You can grow up in a positive household, yet become negative because of tendencies from past lives or influences from the collective, or you can grow up in a negative household, but your past accumulations or other influences are positive. Most of the negativity is connected to karma, or patterns that are part of your individuality.

Let's go down the list and look at each more closely.

1. Feeling too much pressure to complete a project. You are the type of individual who has too much happening in your life. You have the tendency to take on too many projects and then you abandon them out of frustration. Overworked, you are sometimes too preoccupied with the mundane things in life. When projects are not completed, you take on a load of guilt and self-criticism.

2. Feeling that something that you want will never happen for you. The disappointment becomes a steady condition and remains throughout your life, pervading it. Attempts to work toward a goal stop, as the belief system is that no goal can be accomplished. The condition is different from not completing a project; instead, it is an attitude that affects your whole being. The negative thoughts attract negative energies that can entrench this even more deeply.

3. Loss of hope around feelings of love toward someone who does not reciprocate. When someone truly does not return love, you need to drop that person and look for someone who will love you. When you can't stop loving the wrong person, you are immersed in a victim pattern, and you need to look at your childhood conditioning to determine how and when this pattern came about and heal the wound.

4. Not fulfilling goals because of mundane factors. Often the mundane will interfere and not allow you to work toward your goal. An example would be someone who suddenly has to take care of a parent and therefore can't pursue a career. This may cause problems temporarily, but often a different plan can be made to change that impossibility. A very good teacher once said, "Everything is possible, the impossible just takes a little longer."

5. Seeing others' success and feeling discouraged about yourself. This is, again, a negative attitude. If a friend succeeds at something, feel happy for your friend. Ask the friend's advice about the best way for you to move forward. It's also important to look at your patterns. Do you have an unworthiness pattern or a victim pattern? These patterns bring an attitude of failure.

6. **Wanting more than you can have**. This is an attitude of non-acceptance for what you do have. Western society is built on material things, and many people grow up desiring more than is necessary. This is about re-evaluating your life and noticing what you truly need and what isn't necessary. You will be surprised how the latter becomes bigger than the former. If you are someone who needs more all the time, look within to find what you truly need.

7. **Looking at life with dark glasses** is a negative perspective that keeps you from moving forward. If everything is negative, then that attitude will prevail and prohibit expansion and growth. It's important to remain positive even in bad times: this helps make those times change. Always looking at the negative can become part of your personality and prohibit you from enjoying life and what it offers. If you have this attitude at all, really make an effort to look at why you carry it. Notice if your family members have this attitude. It is often learned in childhood.

8. **Having an inner critic that makes you feel unworthy**. Usually this comes from being judged a lot as a child. Realize that the inner critic upsets anything that you do. If you finish a job or a project, the critic will still find fault with it. Often this kind of person is also carrying a perfectionist pattern: everything should be done better, or there is always something that needs to be changed. It's a perpetual nagger that is relentless in its desire for a person to go on trying to improve something when there is no need for improvement. This type of person usually is also critical of others. Such criticism causes inferiority complexes if aimed at children.

9. **Seeing yourself in a negative manner** relates to the inner critic. There will always be an inner critic when you feel this way about yourself. This pattern comes with an inner need to be better, a belief that there are things that you should improve, whether that relates to your personal appearance or to the work you do. You are never satisfied with yourself. Being negative about yourself can be connected to any area in your life. It doesn't necessarily mean you have a sound reason to feel this way. It often is an extreme. For example, if you feel you have to exercise every day and you fail to do so one day, then you will be upset with yourself for a long time. The self-judgment is followed with, "I should have done so and so." The shoulds

are very much a part of the thinking process. It's best to accept what you do or don't do and not go to that extreme, which borders on fanaticism.

10. **Last but not least is looking at the future with no enthusiasm**. This implies that you have nothing to look forward to. Generally, someone like this has given up on life and is resolved to just live day by day in a state of boredom. People who have little impact on others and have very few friends are often in this category. They never seek to learn more or to grow wiser. Their main focus is to vegetate in a lonely world, always to just do the same things day after day. If you are like this, you will benefit from simply changing the routines you follow. Plan to be adventurous and do something new that is interesting. Were there examples of people like this in your family? If so, you may have picked up this conditioning.

Exercise:

> *Go through each of the above and rate yourself from one to ten, ten being the highest level of having that characteristic or attitude. Then prioritize your list and start working with the one that you rated as the highest. Ask yourself the following questions about it:*
> *Have I always had this, or did it develop more recently?*
> *If you have always had it, reflect on your childhood, asking what caused it to start.*
> *If it is a more recent pattern, ask what brought it into being.*
> *Then connect with your heart and ask: Is there another cause for my having this characteristic or attitude?*
> *If the answer is yes, ask: What is it?.*
> *If you believe in reincarnation, ask your Higher Self: Is this characteristic or attitude something I brought in from a past life?*
> *If the answer is yes, ask if you could see more of that life.*
> *Finally, ask your Higher Self for a process and a first step in changing the characteristic or attitude. Begin to work with this first step.*

If you believe in reincarnation, realize that some of these attitudes can come from past lives and often are engrained in your psyche, affecting your thought patterns, which in turn affect your personality. Trying to find the source of an attitude or characteristic can help you in trying to change it.

If it is a pattern you brought with you, it will be more difficult to change. Realize that such patterns can pull you into karmic situations that in turn enhance the pattern. The wheel of karma is a very intricate one that takes time and understanding to balance.

As you begin your work with this exercise, also add a nightly review in which you look back on the day and notice if you were using the pattern during the day. Recognize the kind of situations that cause it to arise so that you can be more aware when you are in a similar situation in the future. Awareness helps you to stop the pattern and change the attitude.

Exercise:

> *Go through the process of connecting with your heart center.*
> *Then take the attitude you are starting to work with and ask the following questions:*
> *Is there anything I can do to have more awareness of when I am in this attitude?*
> *What undercurrents exist around this pattern?*
> *When I am in this pattern, how can I have the awareness to stop it?*
> *Is there anything else I should do to change it in addition to the Higher Self's original suggestion?*

The more you work with changing an attitude, the stronger the pressure to remain in it can become. Be aware that your lower nature will keep fighting you to try to keep you in the negative attitude.

Negative attitudes often keep someone from working with the heart. Instead of being in the heart, the person is only in the mind, and when someone is operating out of the mind, that person is more prone to being influenced by the lower nature. When you do your nightly review, notice whether your mind was fully operating when you were in an attitude or characteristic. If that was the case, take time to connect with your heart and replay the situation in your imagination: see how it might have gone had you been in your heart, noticing especially the difference in the attitude. Then begin trying to consciously switch to being in your heart in your daily life.

The lower nature is caught up in holding a person in a negative pattern. When you recognize the pattern then you can understand how it can control your life. These patterns grow and expand with use, especially if they aren't noticed right away. Don't be discouraged if you suddenly become aware of a particularly strong pattern. Realize that it is something that is strong in your unconscious and affects your behavior when you are least aware of it, and know that this pattern can be changed.

A person's personality can be changed with the use of the heart. When you feel you have said something harsh or wrong to someone, always apologize—do it inside yourself if the person is no longer living or if for some other reason it's not possible—and then imagine what you would have said and the manner in which you would have said it had you been in your heart. The more you work with your heart on a daily basis, the more easily you will change these negative attitudes and patterns.

If you find an attitude is difficult to change, ask your Higher Self why you want to hold on to it. There may be unconscious motivations that you aren't aware of. And always remember: change can happen.

Part Two: Relating to Others

7

Using the Heart to Mirror Others

The heart is a wonderful instrument, but like any instrument, it needs to be practiced to achieve its full potential.

One of the most important ways to use the heart is to listen with the heart and hear what another person is really saying. This means to listen, not only to the words that are being expressed, but also to the thoughts and feelings that are not being expressed.

When you listen to someone, often you may feel the person is leaving something out, something that is very important to the conversation. That can come from several sources. The person may not be in touch with his true feelings, or the person may have some fears around saying what he truly feels. There could also be a resistance to having the truth revealed, so he may feel it best to not say certain things.

For example, someone may need to tell you about a situation that could affect you, but the person doesn't want to reveal too much, as the information was told to him in confidence. He simply wants to alert you. Or perhaps someone feels something intuitively but doesn't want to express it in case he is mistaken about the feeling. This protects him from being wrong. Many times a friend wants to help but doesn't know the right way to offer help. Certain people do not want to hurt anyone's feelings so will not come out and say what is bothering them.

So how do you use your heart to help the person be more honest, or simply to help the person get more in touch with his true feelings? First, you need to relate to the person in a disidentified manner. If you have strong opinions about something, you are not going to be able to mirror the person to understand his feelings. There can be no attachment to the outcome. You may want to help him, but if you are attached to his accepting your help, you will not be disidentified and will not know with your heart what he needs most.

The main thing to remember is that you want to listen in a disidentified manner, with no personal emotions, opinions, or needs arising in the conversation.

In relating to others, here are some of the things to be aware of:

1. Making someone realize that you understand and feel what he is going through.

2. Keeping silent about your awareness when your heart tells you that it would be interfering.

3. Looking at methods to gently help someone.

4. Being positive even though your heart tells you that the person has serious problems.

5. Making the person comfortable in revealing secrets to you. This means he can trust your confidentiality.

6. Helping someone look within for his own answers.

7. Guiding someone to seek help elsewhere.

8. Not being attached to your opinions or feelings about being correct.

9. Trying to simply be there as a sounding board for someone who needs only that.

10. Giving encouragement to someone to do what he feels he needs to do, even though you may not agree with him.

11. Helping someone who is feeling overwhelmed to simply look at each thing one at a time.

12. Being aware when someone is afraid to talk, and accepting that decision by not trying to force him to do so.

13. Making the commitment to help someone without strings attached.

14. Not becoming attached to any outcome.

15. Trying to stay clear of your own projections.

16. Using your understanding to only help someone.

17. Not making your own understanding important.

18. Listening to another without judgment.

19. Not trying to solve another's problems. Instead, helping him solve them for himself.

20. Being loving at all times.

Exercise:

> *Look over the above list and mark those items that you honestly feel are going to be difficult for you to follow. Assess this by placing the statement in your heart and asking: Can I do this fully? If you feel the answer is no, ask yourself why, and then try to come to a better understanding of the why.*

Link with your heart to help you with this, but be aware that if a statement is a problem for you, you may have to go deeper to understand why. For example, you may feel you cannot let go of an opinion you have around another person's problem, mainly because you have known about it for a long time and have formed opinions about what the person should do. In such a case, a way to prepare yourself before meeting with this person is to imagine your opinions written on a blackboard and then see yourself erasing them. At the same time, tell yourself, "I will not bring these into the conversation. I will just listen to how he is feeling, and respond according to what I feel he needs to hear from me."

This approach may be very different from what you previously would have done, but going into the conversation with an open heart allows you to pick up more of what the other person is feeling and what he needs for support. Your previous opinion may not be what he needs to hear.

Often a person expresses sympathy toward a friend who is having troubles, but maybe the best thing the friend needs from you is not sympathy but direct confrontation. Compassion comes through in many ways, not just by being kind and sweet. A person may sometimes need straight talk that is strong and not necessarily kind. If your heart is open and you are disidentified from your own material, you will know exactly what the person needs and can help that person according to his needs, not yours. Here is a story that illustrates this:

Many years ago in a small village there was a woman named Louise who lived alone in a cottage near the woods at the edge of the village. As she grew older, she became more nervous about being isolated and perhaps a prey for robbers or bandits. Before this, she'd lived there with her son, who had died suddenly, leaving her by herself at the age of seventy-five.

A relative advised her to sell her home and move to a smaller place in the heart of town where she would be more protected. Louise knew this was a good idea, but she had lived her whole married life in her cottage, and she still enjoyed the quiet of living near the woods and being sheltered by old beautiful trees.

She also had a heart condition and knew that if something happened and she had a heart attack, it would be difficult for help to reach her in time.

In her dilemma, she spoke with her closest friends, who all advised her to sell and move into town, where they all lived. The idea of moving made her increasingly depressed, but she didn't know what else to do.

One day, Louise was walking back from town with a few groceries on her arm when she encountered an old man seated under a tree, resting. She could see that he looked tired and was feeling the heat. She offered him some water, which she had with her as it was a hot day. He thanked her and said, "Please join me here under the tree. You could use a rest also."

She did so, and he then said, "I've seen you in town once in a while. Where do you live?"

"I live at the end of this road by the forest, but I am going to have to sell my cottage now that I am old, and move into town."

He could tell that she was not happy about doing this, so he said, "That's too bad. I'm sure it has many memories for you. How long have you lived there?"

"Many years, and you're right, it has wonderful memories that I can't bring with me. I can bring the furniture, but the cottage itself and the woods, I have to leave behind." Her voice cracked with emotion.

"That is sad to hear. Maybe there is another solution to this problem."

"I can't think of any. It's pretty basic."

"Is there someone who could come and live with you and keep you company?"

"No, I only have a distant relative who doesn't want to leave her home, and the same is true of my remaining close friends. They want me to move to town and be closer to them."

The man, whose name was Lionel, thought for a few minutes, then said, "You know, I have seen some young girls who look like they live on the streets. And there is one in particular, a nice girl around twelve years old, who is constantly begging for food to eat. Why not adopt her? She could help you in your old age and be there for you if you become ill. I asked her once where her parents were. She said she had none, but she lived with an aunt who insisted that she beg for her own food and who she does a lot of work for."

"I have never thought about doing anything like that. But would she want to take care of an old woman like me?"

"Why not ask her? I think it would be a much better situation than she is in now. She told me her aunt was very mean to her. Let me speak to her first, and if she is interested, I will bring her back here to meet you."

While Louise sat and waited for him to return, she thought about having a young girl in her life and she started to feel excited. She had always wanted a daughter but had only had one son. Maybe it would work.

Lionel came back with the girl, whose name was Anna. She appeared uncertain and shy. When Louise saw her, she loved her at once, and soon they were talking about the cottage and her life. She invited Anna to come home with her and see it for herself, which she did.

When Louise turned to thank the man, he smiled and said, "Now, you can be happy again."

Anna moved in with Louise and they lived a quiet, happy life together. When Louise died, Anna stayed on in the cottage, which Louise had left to her, and eventually married and had a family of her own there.

Lionel was in town just for a short time. He continued his journey going from town to town, helping others as much as he could. He had an open heart and knew how to use it.

The heart has the inspiration to see many solutions to problems, whereas the mind often only sees one. If the situation had not worked out for Louise with Anna, Lionel would have come up with another solution, because he was experiencing her need to stay in her home. If she had moved into town, she would have died soon after, as her need to live in beautiful surroundings was too strong to have withstood the town's ugliness and vibrations.

Sometimes a practical person becomes totally focused on the practicalities of the mind, not realizing that a different solution from the obvious one could be better. When you can let go of what you think should happen and instead ask your heart, you may be surprised at the outcome.

Exercise:

Think about a problem that you may have with someone else. Make it a problem that you feel but have not been able to express to the person. Think about what you need to say to the person. In fact, go over the whole scenario. You would say this, and what would the person say in return, etc. Play it out as to how it would end.

Now, instead of working with your mind, put the problem in your heart and ask your heart what would be the best way to approach the person. What words would the heart express and what does your heart feel would be the response from the other person? Notice the different conclusions or different dialogues that would happen if you used your heart instead of your mind. If you feel the heart approach may work better, then try it. When you feel ready to try it, be careful to always respond from your heart, not the mind or the emotions. If you feel you may get more personal and can't stay in

> *your heart, then wait until you feel your emotions can*
> *be put aside so that you can only be in your heart.*

Working with your heart takes practice. Do not feel upset if at first you get emotional and cannot follow through with your heart. Try again, and start to feel the difference when you can remain disidentified and in your heart. It takes time, work and concentration to mirror someone.

Exercise:

> *Make a list of your friends, and mark the names of*
> *those whom you feel you can do the mirroring exercise*
> *with. Choose people with whom you do not have strong*
> *emotions.*

The people closest to you may be difficult to work with right away, so start with those with whom you feel more disidentifed. Experiment with them first, and only when you feel more certain about the process should you try to do it with someone who is more challenging for you. Take time with this, as it requires time to feel the difference.

If you have work associates, they may be the best people to start with, unless the work is very mind-oriented; then you could be using the mind more.

Before you meet with someone, read the list from earlier in this chapter about relating to others. That will help you remember to be disidentified. After the meeting, check back to see if you tried to mirror the person and if that was successful.

When you have been successful, acknowledge yourself. Feel how good it is to use your heart in this manner.

One last thing to remember: when you mirror someone, always link your Higher Self to the other person's Higher Self, asking that you mirror him in the conversation. The other person's Higher Self will thus be connected to yours and can send whatever is appropriate for your heart to understand about the person at that time.

8

Why Some Relationships Don't Work

This chapter will look at what is needed to have a good working relationship with another person. Often a relationship is one-sided, meaning one of the people involved is good about helping the other person but the other person neglects to reciprocate. Not only is such a relationship one-sided, but also, generally, it then falls into the category of being an acquaintance and not a close relationship.

To have a truly close relationship with another person, you both need to have the following:

- The desire to see each other on a regular basis, and if you can't do this, then the desire to talk to each other via telephone or Skype.

- The need to relate information to each other, information that is new and exciting.

- The need to help each other when help is needed.

- Generally, the need to share feelings and emotions.

- The hope that your friend will support you in the work you are doing.

- Wanting to fulfill your friend's desires if it's possible to do so.

- Caring about how your friend is feeling, especially if she has been sick.

- Looking at your friend always in a positive manner.

- Seeing the negative but never dwelling on that, but rather emphasizing the positive.

- When your friend is having a problem, being there to listen from the heart.

- Keeping your friend updated on what is happening in your life, whether it is good or bad.

- If you go through a loss of any kind, trusting your friend will be there to support you.

- Knowing you can rely on your friend for help of any kind.

- Knowing that your friend is someone you can call at any time of the day or evening.

- Expecting your friendship to last forever.

- Knowing your friend will support any major decision in your life, whether she agrees with it or not.

- Feeling your friend is family.

- Wanting to be with your friend during difficult times.

- Hoping your friend will always be strong and healthy.

- Seeing your friendship as indispensable.

All of the above can apply in most close relationships.

Exercise:

Make a list of all the people you consider close friends. Taking each name, go through the above list of requirements and evaluate each statement as it applies to your relationship, rating it from one to ten: ten representing the closest that the statement applies. Generally, a good relationship should rate high on the requirements, and if it doesn't, maybe you need to reevaluate the friendship. If you find it one-sided on any items, then try to understand what you need to do to achieve more positive ratings.

Even a romantic relationship should contain most of the above, only with some more intimate needs added to the list. But whether the friendship is platonic or romantic, hopefully the above statements will apply. Sometimes a romantic relationship can work for a while without the kind of mutual support required in a close relationship, but as the excitement of the romance fades, there needs to be a good, basic friendship in order for the relationship to continue. If that is not there, the relationship will end.

It's good to see a relationship in a different light from a romantic affair. Sex always adds a layer that can smother other vital needs.

When you enter a romantic relationship, try first to check if the person would be someone you could also have a close friendship with. Is the person capable of the listed requirements, or is she too self-centered to be able to meet them?

Unfortunately, romance often hides the true character of someone. If your sexual needs are met then it's easier to overlook the other relationship needs. Try to establish these other needs first, before jumping into any sexual involvement. If you don't know the person well, you can still intuitively feel whether this person could someday be someone you would have a close relationship with. Find out if the person has any close friends, or does she mainly have acquaintances? Test her on some items in the list: for example, if you are feeling sick, does she offer to help you? If you need to take your car in for repairs and must leave it there, does she offer to pick you up and drive you for the time needed? Or, if you ask her, does she agree, or does she say that she's too busy?

It's wise to build some boundaries in a relationship. When you do that, you make it clear to your friend what your needs are, and your friend should also make clear to you what her needs are. Boundaries really define needs, and in making them clear, you are more aware of what each of you hopes from the other. She may need a great deal more than you want to give. Setting boundaries will clarify that right away.

Relationships should not be based just on fulfilling another person's needs. You want to be there for a friend, but you don't want the friend to expect you to fulfill her needs. That would only cause a dependency, and dependency is not positive for a relationship. The following story illustrates this.

> Isabel was a quiet, attractive woman in her late
> thirties. She met a woman who was ten years older,
> and soon they became close friends. The woman, Al-
> ice, was married to an international banker who trav-

eled a lot for his business. Alice hated to travel so she rarely went with him. Their two children were both in college, so Alice found herself living alone most of the time. Isabel was someone she had a lot in common with, and they quickly formed a close friendship and spent a lot of time together. Isabel was divorced, with no children, and at the time hadn't found another man to have a romantic relationship with.

Alice became more and more dependent on Isabel, and Isabel, though she liked her, was starting to feel a bit overwhelmed by her demands. It was as if Alice needed to be with her every day, or at least talk to her daily. Isabel started to back away and didn't have the courage to sit down with Alice and tell her how she was feeling; instead, she didn't return all the phone calls, and she started telling Alice she was busy.

One evening she bumped into Alice in a store. She had told Alice she was busy that night because she was meeting friends for dinner, when in fact she was out shopping on her own. Alice was furious and screamed at her in the store for having lied to her. Isabel was so embarrassed she didn't know what to do. She spoke to another friend about what had happened, and her friend stated she needed to confront Alice about her behavior and maybe even end the friendship.

Isabel felt bad about this. She did like Alice a lot and hoped to keep her as a friend, so she got up her courage, sat down with her and told her honestly how she was feeling. Alice realized that Isabel was correct and that she had been too demanding. Mainly she realized that instead of confronting her husband about how little time he was spending with her, she was using Isabel as a scapegoat for her anger toward her husband. They set up some boundaries, and Isabel talked Alice into confronting her husband. When she did so, he agreed that he had been too busy to be with her, and he let her know he missed their relationship also. He needed to continue to travel a lot, but Alice agreed to accompany him on his longer trips, and she even began to enjoy them more than she thought she would.

In the meantime, Isabel realized she needed to find a romantic relationship of her own and started to look for someone.

Isabel and Alice's relationship changed and developed into a true friendship based on sharing, with no demands. It continued to last even after Isabel married again, and then the two couples socialized together.

If Isabel hadn't confronted Alice and had simply broken off the relationship, that would have been a shame, as there was a good foundation for them to become good friends in a positive way.

Often friendships end because of misunderstandings that are never discussed. When that happens, it causes a feeling of loss on both people's parts, and in that loss, a questioning of what one could have done differently. If something arises in a relationship, it's important to discuss it before it becomes something deeper and causes feelings of antipathy. Hopefully when misunderstandings happen they can be cleared up quickly, but in some cases, it's important to understand what went wrong in the first place. When you have a friendship that ends for one reason or another, it's important to understand the course of events that caused it to end.

Exercise:

> *Think back on your life and write down a list of people you used to be good friends with, but then the friendship ended or changed into an acquaintance. Take each name on your list and ask yourself the following questions about the relationship:*
> *Did we share our true feelings?*
> *If the answer is yes, ask: Did it feel comfortable to share?*
> *If the answer is no, ask: Why not?*
> *Was there any dependency in the relationship?*
> *If the answer is yes, ask: What was the dependency about and how did it make me feel?*
> *Did you feel that this person was someone who was there for you in any case scenario?*
> *If the answer is yes, ask: How did that make me feel?*

If the answer is no, ask: How did that make me feel?
What do you think was the true cause of the breakup?
Could that have been different? And if so, what needed
to happen?
Would you like to try having a close relationship with
this person again?
If the answer is yes, ask: How should I pursue this?
If the answer is no, ask: Why not? Then look at the why
not and let yourself feel whether that's correct.
If it feels correct, accept that this had to be the outcome.
If it doesn't feel correct, ask yourself: Could there still be
another outcome?

In general, having a good relationship requires work. For those who believe in past lives, sometimes a lot of feelings are founded in those. Most karmic relationships at the beginning have positive feelings. If there is hidden negative karma, it won't come out immediately, but eventually it will appear, bringing negative feelings that can change the relationship from a positive one to a negative one and causing the relationship to end. If you can be aware of this happening and understand the reason, then you can let go of the past and continue to develop a positive relationship with the person, which will offset the negative karma.

Even if you don't believe in karma, it's important to realize where the negative feelings are coming from and whether they are founded in truth or simply on a misunderstanding that can be discussed and rectified. Being open with someone is always the best way to be in any relationship. This can be a problem for many people. A person who has a difficult time being open about her feelings will generally keep burying them until they grow out of proportion. Then when they come out, a lot of hurt and misunderstanding happens, and as a consequence, the relationship ends. Most often, if the issue had been discussed right away, it could have easily been resolved.

If you are someone who can't discuss a problem immediately, try the following exercise.

Exercise:

Put the question in your heart and ask:
Why am I afraid to discuss problems with a friend?
Does my fear have anything to do with my childhood
conditioning?

If the answer is yes, ask: What happened in my child-
hood to cause this?
If the answer is no, ask: What then keeps me from being
open with my feelings?
How can I change this fear and become more open with
my friends? Give me a process and a first step.
Now imagine yourself doing the first step. How does it
feel?
If it doesn't feel comfortable, ask: How can I change my
feeling of not being comfortable doing this?
Then, work on changing the feeling before trying the
first step again.

If you have difficulty talking to someone directly about what you are feeling, you may have to try doing it in baby steps. If your childhood conditioning kept you from expressing yourself, then it will be more difficult to suddenly change that pattern. If this is the case, ask yourself the following questions:

If I tried to express myself as a child, what were the
consequences?
Do I feel that those same consequences would happen
now if I fully expressed myself?
What would be the best small step to take?

If you can't come up with an answer to this, ask your Higher Self this question.

Next, it would be helpful for you to choose a good friend with whom to try the baby step. Pick someone to whom you can explain what you are doing so that the person can be supportive of you. Also, try to pick someone you feel has an easy time expressing herself.

After you have done the first step, ask your Higher Self for a second step, and so on, until you feel comfortable in being more open with people. Then, look at the list of people with whom you have broken friendships, and if there is anyone you'd like to resume a good relationship with, try calling that person and having an open talk with her.

Not being able to express yourself is usually a problem for everyone. It takes practice, and sometimes it just doesn't work. You also have to decide whether or not the person you need to be open with will in turn be open with you. It can't be one-sided, and if it is, then it's not a real conversation.

Sometimes your intuition will tell you that it's best not to try to talk to the person, so follow that. But be certain it's your intuition that is telling you this and not some inner fear that you will be rejected if you try.

Take time to understand the real cause of your inability to confront the person. Is it based on reality, or is it something in you that is causing it? For example, if the person has hurt your feelings and you still feel the hurt, then it will be more difficult to confront her concerning how you feel. It may be better, in that case, to wait until your feelings have subsided, so you can be more centered and disidentified when you talk to her.

Understandably, if you have someone in your life who is always saying hurtful things to you, then you most definitely need to confront that person and ask her why she is doing this. If she can't change this behavior, you would be better off ending the relationship. This is also true if the relationship is a romantic one.

It's more difficult in the case of a close relative or a spouse's relative. You can't easily break off the relationship, so you have to live with it being the way it is unless you really talk to the person about it. If the person is an in-law, this becomes more difficult. In this case, you need to first talk to your spouse about the best way to resolve the situation. If she feels you can't resolve it, then look at that advice and decide if it is correct. Mainly, you shouldn't continue to be abused by a person, no matter what her relationship is in the family. It's wrong behavior, and if you take this kind of treatment, then you are put into what is called a victim pattern.

Exercise:

>*Put the following questions in your heart and ask:*
>*Do I in any way have a victim pattern?*
>*If the answer to that question is yes, then ask: Does it come from a past life?*
>*If you don't believe in past lives, ask: Where does the pattern come from?*
>*Then ask for a process and a first step in trying to stop being in this pattern.*

Friendship is very important for everyone. If you find that you have very few close friends, then you need to ask yourself why you haven't tried to cultivate more. It's never too late. Look at the people you know as acquaintances. Is there anyone you would like to develop a closer relationship with? If so, make a point to start doing that. But if there isn't anyone that you care to develop that with, then plan to socialize more and try to meet people who could be new friends.

Relating to Others

Using Information Correctly that Comes through the Heart

The heart has the ability to intuitively understand someone and use that information positively to help the person. Unfortunately, personal desires can sometimes interfere in this process. For example, you may feel a friend needs help, so you try to help the friend, but you also have the desire of wanting something in return. Or you may be attracted to the person and helping him may be the best way to get him to notice you. This kind of help, then, has an attachment to it, and the person being helped usually feels that demand and doesn't feel comfortable with your help. The altruistic attempt is there, but it gets clouded with individual desires.

To genuinely follow the heart's desire to help with no strings attached is a goal to have, but it can take practice to truly be able to do this.

Sometimes, if you help someone, you may believe that the person owes you a favor and should help you in return when you need help. This is an expectation that is not part of your heart. It comes from your personal desires and works through your heart in a negative manner.

Information coming through your heart concerning someone you know needs to be received when you are feeling disidentified, so that you can truly feel in your heart that the information is true. Only then can you use it to help the person or to just be there for the person in a positive manner.

Sometimes you may pick up something that feels important to convey, but always double-check by putting the information back into your heart and asking for verification. Also, if the information is something around which you have any desire, it needs to be tested out: for example, you may feel that your heart is telling you that a person you just met is very attracted to you. The person may not have pursued a relationship, but you have a feeling that he would like to. If this is your desire, and not the other person's, and you follow your own feeling by contacting the person and pursuing him, that may be a wrong action. To test out your feeling that he would like a relationship, it would be better to wait to see if he calls you or to go to a social event that he will be at and speak with him there. If you do this, be certain to try to be disidentifed so that you can truly feel whether or not he is indeed interested.

Psychics have a tendency to predict things that a person wants to hear. They pick things up and often feel they are right when actually they are just listening to the desires of the person. The person thinks that the psychic has to be correct as it's an inner desire that no one knows about.

Another example is a mother who wants her child to excel and overwhelms him with all kinds of activities that the child doesn't really want to do. Telling the mother that this is wrong won't work, as she thinks she is doing the best thing for her child. In the old days, a male child had to follow in the career path of his father. This was expected even if the child hated that kind of work and was not suited for the vocation. Many people at that time did work they hated their whole lives.

It's always important to verify information you receive when you are meditating, or even when you are dreaming, as your desires can also be active in dreams.

To determine how accurate the information is that you receive through your heart, do the following:

Exercise:

> *Ask your Higher Self the following questions:*
> *Can I trust what my heart tells me most of the time?*
> *If the answer is no, ask: Is there a specific area that I*
> *have to be careful with?*
> *When you receive what that is, ask: How can I best*
> *check out what I receive in this area?*
> *How much of the information given to me is correct?*
> *Is the incorrect information coming from my desires?*

Is the incorrect information coming from my lower nature?
What is my best way to verify information coming through my heart?
When I feel information is incorrect, how do I handle it?
If I am not certain if the information is correct, what do I do?
If I feel the information is correct and I act on it and find out that it's wrong, what do I do?
If I feel the information is correct and I act on it and find out that it's right, is there anything more I need to do?
Can I trust my answers from you?
How can I best check out these answers?

The Higher Self is always correct, but there can be interference from your desires and the lower nature. Generally, it's good to question anything your Higher Self says when it doesn't feel right to you. Also, you can ask the Higher Self the same question again, and if you receive a different answer, realize that something is interfering. Look at the question to see how your desires or your lower nature may be coming in.

The following is a story that illustrates this.

In the old West during the gold rush days in California and Alaska, there was a man named John who took his family in a wagon across the states to find gold. His family consisted of his wife, Emily, and daughter, Ann, who was ten, and a new baby boy named Jasper. It was a tough journey, particularly going through the Indian territories. The wagon caravan was large with at least twenty wagons and lots of men on horses protecting them from Indian raids. Several raids happened, and during one of them, John was fatally wounded, leaving his family alone with no man to protect them.

It was too late to return home, so they continued on with the help and protection of some of the men in the caravan. Thomas, one of these men, was single, and he became interested in Emily and tried to convince her that she needed him and should marry him. Emily felt very desperate and was feeling deep sorrow over her loss of John, whom she really loved. Thomas was nice enough, but her intuition made her feel that he was wrong for her, so she told him that it was too soon after her loss to consider getting married again.

He kept trying to convince her that she had no other choice: Who would take care of her and her children? They all needed him. Even though Emily thought it wrong, she felt helpless in her loss and didn't know what else to do. Besides that, the other families in the caravan tried to convince her that a marriage would end up fine; love was not necessary at first, and Thomas was a good man. So, toward the end of the journey when they entered a small town, the local minister married them.

Emily soon realized what a mistake she had made. Thomas immediately started being demanding and abusive with her and with Ann. She didn't know what to do. The more controlling he became, the more fragile she became, until she finally got very sick and died of pneumonia after their arrival in California. Thomas was left with the two children he didn't want, and he finally found an orphanage in San Francisco that would take them off his hands. Before that, he had sexually assaulted Ann, who was twelve at the time.

Here was a case in which Emily didn't listen to her heart and her intuition. She felt she had no choice, and in those days that seemed to be true. Yet there were other men, even in the caravan, who were interested in her, but Thomas had threatened them to leave her alone. If Emily had said no from the very beginning and stuck with her no, Thomas may have given up and let the other men have a chance. One of them was a very nice older man who would have taken good care of her.

Sometimes friends and family can persuade a person to do something that the person's heart says is wrong. Therefore, it's important to always verify things with your heart and not listen to people who think they are looking out for your best interests but are seeing things with their minds and not their hearts.

Emily's story is the kind of story that takes place not just in the 18th century but also in the present day. Arranged marriages of convenience still exist, and often they involve controlling men with high expectations of being in charge. In the East there are many such marriages that are abusive, with no hope for the women and female children to have happiness.

When you receive information concerning someone else, it's important to understand the way in which you can receive this information. You may want to review this by going to the exercise in Chapter Two.

People who are visual can see a scene in their mind's eye or in their semi-waking state between sleepiness and being fully asleep. They can also have prophetic dreams about someone that will come true. Auditory people hear a sentence or a phrase related to someone that can also be prophetic. These people can also be told something in the waking state or in a dream state. Feeling people can suddenly and intuitively feel emotional about someone and know something is wrong. Lastly, people who are sensory or feel things in their bodies can think about someone and pick up a sensation of what is happening to the person. They can also be prophetic and pick up something before it happens. These people are sensitive to conditions and usually highly intuitive about what they are feeling.

Some people have a combination of these senses and therefore can verify something more easily if they pick something up in one sense and verify it in another. For example, a person may sense something is wrong with a friend and feel it in his body, and then, closing the eyes, see his friend ill or in trouble.

Again, it is important, when you intuit something concerning a person you know, to immediately put the information into your heart and ask if that information is true.

If you doubt anything you receive, just write it down and check whether it eventually comes true. The exception is if you receive a warning about someone else, then it's best to tell the person that you are picking something up that may be true or not and for the person to be careful for a period of time. If you are shown that someone may die, that is one thing you should not tell them. For example, if you receive a warning that someone you know could die in an automobile accident, you don't frighten him by telling him that; instead, you can tell the person to be careful when he drives because he could have an accident. If he follows that advice, he will be more careful when driving and maybe avoid being killed.

You may be a person who doesn't receive things and feel that this chapter is not for you. Most people who feel this way are not taking the time to go to a deep level in the heart. If you start working with your heart energy, you will soon develop the ability to receive things.

Anything you receive for yourself, you need to verify in the same way you do for others. The difference is that you will have more interference on what you intuit about yourself than what you intuit about others. The previous chapter went into how that happens with personal desires in relationships. The same can happen if you have desires around anything else. You may have desires for material things and sense that you will make a lot of money someday. These kinds of desires should be written down and questioned. You also may have a desire for your children to do well financially and see that happening to them. I suggest that you write those observations down also, and don't tell your children, as these intuitions could be coming from your desires.

Exercise:

> *Make a list of all your desires. Really think about whether you are holding onto them. Then, check with your Higher Self to see whether it agrees that you have the desires you have listed. Also, ask the Higher Self if there is anything else you need to add to your list.*

If you pick up an intuition in your heart and even feel you have verified it, you can see if it is on your list, and if so, question it. You can also ask a good friend who you know is intuitive to verify information for you.

Be patient, and know that even though you haven't had this ability, you can certainly develop it. It is a positive ability to have, as it can help you in life and also help your friends and loved ones.

10

When Couples Use Their Hearts Properly

Couples who use the information coming from the heart are couples that have strong, loving relationships. To achieve this is very difficult because it requires a good personal understanding of what knowledge comes directly from the heart and what knowledge is coming from the mind. When you know someone very well, there is usually also a mental understanding, and the mental understanding can get in the way of true heart knowledge.

If you look at couples that have been married thirty years and more, these couples have grown alike. They even begin to look alike. This is because they have learned to adjust and live with each other, not necessarily in a positive manner, but certainly in most cases the adjustment makes their lives easier. You may see a couple that has the same fights and the same routines over and over again, but these fall into place and keep the couple bound to each other.

These couples have adjusted to each other. But how many couples have you seen who have been together for a long time and demonstrate love and affection for each other in a way that shows they are always relating to each other from their hearts? This is rare to see, but when you see it, you know it right away. They may even express their love for each other by never being apart. This is not co-dependence, which is different, but a genuine preference to always be together. Usually, when one person in such a couple dies, the other one dies shortly after. The longing to be with her partner makes that happen.

How does a couple achieve such a relationship after so many years? Obviously, they had to work at learning to accept each other in all the positive and negative aspects of their personalities. True acceptance comes from the heart. It's literally not letting each other's foibles in any way be bothersome. When the love aspect of the relationship is very strong and solid, then achieving this is very possible. Each person has to know in their heart how much the other person means to them.

Let's be honest in this exercise.

Exercise:

> If you are in a relationship at this time, think about your partner and write down all the positive characteristics that she has, and follow that by writing down all the negative characteristics. First, look at the list of positive aspects. Take each aspect, put it into your heart and feel how meaningful that is to you. You may even want to rate each aspect as to how important it is for you. The ratings should be one to ten, ten being the highest in importance. For example, she is very affectionate. This means maybe an eight rating to you. You like her being affectionate most of the time, but not necessarily 100 percent of the time. If you like the 100 percent, you would have made it a ten instead of an eight.
>
> After you have done this, look at your list of all the negative characteristics that she has. Repeat the rating process you did for the previous list. Take each aspect, and rate it in terms of how important it is for you. For example, she has a tendency to talk too much. You rate this a six, as half of the time this bothers you. Go through your list in this way, considering the importance of each characteristic.
>
> Now look at both lists. Do you have more positive characteristics than negative characteristics? And do you have more positive ratings on both lists, or more that could be considered negative?

*Just look at the lists generally, then put both of them in
your heart. How does it feel to hold them in your heart
as you think about the person? Can you have a heartfelt
relationship with this person? Can you accept all of her
negative aspects completely, or are there some you still
cannot accept? These are the ones you need to recognize
at this time and put on a separate list to work on.*

The separate list should contain those characteristics that you cannot
completely accept. They are the ones that keep bothering you over and
over again, and probably they are the ones you end up fighting about with
your partner. Let's look at these more carefully.

*Take each characteristic one at a time and ask yourself
the following questions:
Can I have a clear, non-judgmental discussion with my
partner about this characteristic that bothers me about
her?
If the answer is yes, then ask yourself: What would be
the best way to approach her?
Also ask: When I approach her, can I do so with an
open heart that listens to her?
If the answer is no, then ask yourself: How can I best try
to resolve this within myself so that it doesn't bother me
as much as it does?
Also ask: Do I have this characteristic inside me?
If the answer is yes, ask: How can I start to eliminate it
within me?
If I have this characteristic, do I in any way project it
onto my partner?*

After you have gone through your list, check your answers and observations in your heart to see if what you have written is correct and, also,
whether there is something you have forgotten or not observed that needs
to be added.

Often what bothers you the most is something you have within yourself, and it is very natural to not see it clearly in yourself but instead let it
magnify in your partner because you are projecting it onto her.

If you feel you can approach your partner, really be certain you are in
your heart and can be open to what she tells you. If you see her becoming

defensive, back off and send her love. Mainly, do not in any way attack her for the characteristic. It's also better to start off such a conversation complimenting her on a positive attribute. Therefore, before having the conversation, look at your list of positive aspects and pick one or two you want to mention before talking about the one you want to resolve. Also, do not talk about several of the characteristics that you feel are negative: stick to one at a time.

Realize that there are also negative characteristics that you have that may bother her. Ask her about those, and let her know that you would also like to work on something that bothers her.

Maybe mention that you would like to have your relationship heart-centered at all times. And mention that you really love her, if that is the case, and that it's important for you that your relationship grow and be very positive.

What I am talking about is not easy to do, particularly if you have already established some negative patterns with each other. Both of you will need to recognize that you each have to make the effort to change and accept more fully the individuality that each of you brings to the relationship.

The following is a story that illustrates what I am talking about.

A married couple who had been together for over forty years decided to go on a vacation to Italy. Both of them were from Italian backgrounds but had never visited the country before. The wife's name was Gene and her husband was Tony. They had two children and several grandchildren. Their life together had been happy, without much stress. It was fairly normal: raising their own children, and taking care of some of the grandchildren when they were older. Unfortunately, they had never done much traveling together. Both were at-home people who loved to entertain, and when they traveled, it generally was to see family or friends who had moved away.

This was their second trip to Europe. They had been on a previous trip many years before to England to see friends who had moved there.

In general, their marriage was good, with just a few ups and downs. Tony had a brief affair earlier in their marriage, but Gene had basically forgiven him and stayed faithful during those years. Still, they were not in the category of loving each other deeply, or even being in their hearts much with each other. They had small spats over simple things, which became part of their normal routine. Theirs had become a marriage of endurance, not an active marriage of affection and love as described earlier in this chapter.

Their journey to Italy was a long, tiring one, and both arrived in a bad mood. They were traveling with a tour group, and the trip they had picked was one that covered a lot of places. The first stop was Rome. There was little time for them to rest. Almost immediately after arriving at their hotel, the sightseeing tour began. By the time they returned to their hotel, their moods had worsened.

"I can't stand the people on this tour, and that goes for our guide too," Gene commented.

"You always have to complain. You never like anybody, and if you keep this up no one will like you either." Tony went into the bathroom and closed the door in disgust.

Then the argument began. When they turned their backs to each other in bed, both were exhausted and feeling sick.

The next day, Gene stayed in the hotel and rested and Tony went with the group and had a good time.

When he returned to the room, Gene was up and packing.

"What are you doing? We don't leave Rome yet."

"I'm leaving. I hate this tour already, and from the little I've seen of Rome, it's ugly."

"How can you say that? You've seen very little of it. Today was great. At least stay for the last day here, and then we go to Orvieto, which is supposed to be lovely. Please, dear, we've always wanted to come here. Give it a chance," he pleaded.

"All right, I will give it two more days, but if I still don't like it I'm going home."

They toured the next day and then drove through some beautiful countryside to Orvieto. The city was small and lovely, with a beautiful black and white stone cathedral. Tony did his best to be cheerful, hoping that his uplifted spirits would change Gene's disposition. Unfortunately, that did not happen. She looked at everything, and even talked to a couple of the people, but generally she was in a negative mood. When she wasn't complaining about something, she was simply looking upset and not at ease.

After the second day in Orvieto, she said to Tony, "I gave it my best and I still don't like being on this tour. I'm leaving and going home."

"If you want to be that way you can, but I'm not leaving. I'm enjoying the trip."

"Naturally, you would enjoy it. I've seen you looking at all the beautiful Italian women. It's pretty obvious that I'm a hindrance."

"That's not true. I've been very attentive to you. It's all your imagination."

Then the fight started, and naturally she brought up their past history when he was unfaithful to her. The people in the room next to theirs knocked on the wall when it started to get late. Only that stopped the fight.

Gene left on her own the next day, making arrangements to return to Rome. The guide was able to change her flight to an earlier one.

On the train going back, a handsome Italian man sat down next to her and they started a conversation. Giovanni was around her age, very charming, and his English was beautiful, with a faint Italian accent that made it lovely to hear. When she explained about the tour, he seemed to understand, remarking that he always disliked tours himself. She also explained that her husband was still on the tour. Since she had a couple of days in Rome awaiting her flight, he asked if he could give her a private tour of the city. He had lived there most of his life and knew some lovely places off the tourist route.

Gene asked Giovanni if he was married and he said yes, but his wife was visiting one of their children in the north for several days.

So it was arranged that after work in the morning, he would pick her up and they would spend the afternoon sightseeing and have dinner together.

It was a lovely day. He not only took her to some very interesting places but he also knew a great deal about the history; it was like having her own personal guide. In the evening they drove a little way out of the city to a small villa where they dined in an elegant setting. When they returned to her hotel, she invited him into the bar room for a nightcap. There, he held her hand and told her how lovely she was. And indeed, she felt lovely.

The next day they spent the day together again, and he invited her to his home where he made her a lovely dinner. His apartment overlooked the Tiber River, with an outline of the Vatican dome in the distance. They had drinks on the balcony and watched the sun set over the water. It was very romantic, and when he tried to kiss her, she responded easily. They continued to kiss until he picked her up and carried her into the bedroom. There, they made passionate love. It was marvelous for her. He was a wonderful lover, and it had been a long time since she had felt anything when making love with Tony. In fact, their lovemaking occurred less and less in recent years. Suddenly, with Giovanni, she felt like a woman again.

He asked her to change her reservations and stay a few days longer. He wanted to take her for a drive down the Almalfi Coast and to stay a couple of nights on the isle of Capri. It sounded wonderful to her and she agreed.

Both spoke only a little about their spouses. She knew that Tony would be calling her when he returned to Rome, so she called her number at home and changed her message, saying she was home but out visiting friends and that she would call him in a couple of days.

Giovanni's wife wasn't expected home for another week, so he could easily call her during the day even when he was with Gene, who couldn't understand Italian.

It worked out very well. The next few days were, again, magical ones. They went to the Isle of Capri and even swam in the beautiful blue water in the grotto there, as the weather was sunny and warm. Then they drove down the coast and stayed in Positano, an exquisite town that was built from the sea in tiers up the side of the hill. They stopped to see the ruins of Pompeii on the way back. The physical passion was still there between them, even with more intensity.

When the trip ended and it was time for her to leave, she looked at him and asked, "Do you want me to stay?"

His reply was, "Well, no, my wife is returning tomorrow, but it was wonderful to be with you. If you come again, let me know. Maybe I can be free to spend some time with you." He smiled at her and kissed her goodbye, but the kiss was distant, and she thought, *this is the end.*

It was just a fling on his part. Then, for the first time, she thought, *How could I have done this to Tony? And then, What happened to us that I could have done this?* She began to realize the part she played in their life, and how she not only took him for granted but never appreciated who he was or how he could be feeling; especially now, alone on a trip that had been so important to both of them.

Instead of taking her plane back, she changed her reservation and looked at her itinerary. The tour was now in Venice. She took a flight there and went to the hotel. The group had just returned from the day's tour and everyone was resting in their rooms before dinner. When Tony saw her, he was very surprised and happy. She embraced him and said, "I realized how wrong I was. Please forgive me. I decided to come back and spend this last amount of time here with you. I think we should extend our trip to see more and maybe go to Paris. But mainly, I want to tell you how much I love you and have always loved you."

Tony responded, "I've been thinking a lot about our marriage and how we have come to a place of taking each other for granted. In the course of doing that we have lost the love and affection that we had in the early years. I would like us to try to bring that back and also not to argue over stupid things. I love you too, and I want us to spend the rest of our lives having fun, being together and mainly, being happy."

Gene kissed him again, and her heart felt full of love and appreciation for who he was.

They continued their journey in Europe and in life, and they indeed changed the behaviors that had driven them apart. Gene never told Tony about her affair with Giovanni. She felt it would hurt him too much, as she had been hurt by his affair. She realized that both affairs no longer mattered. She needed hers to help her realize how much she loved Tony, and it helped her to let go of the resentment she had been carrying for years about his being unfaithful.

One of the things they established in their marriage was setting boundaries. In doing so, they could let go of some of the criticism they had toward one another. They learned to accept the things they disliked in one another, and also they tried harder to correct those things that greatly disturbed one another. Mainly, they were more loving, and this also led to a better and more fulfilling sex life.

Exercise:

If you have a partner, ask yourself the following questions:
Have I set boundaries with my partner, and has my partner set boundaries with me?
When I feel any irritation with my partner, can I easily let it go?
Do I have any unresolved issues with my partner?

When I am with my partner, do I try to always listen
and be disidentified from what she is saying?
Do I genuinely enjoy being with my partner most of the
time?
Am I affectionate and loving toward my partner?
If my partner is upset or ill, can I be helpful and caring?
When I am alone with my partner, am I attentive?
Generally, does my partner fulfill my desires?
When I am with my partner, do I always experience my
love for her?
If you have answered no to any of the above questions,
then ask yourself why you have said no, and also ask
yourself how to change the no to a yes.

Partnerships of any kind take work and often bring out the best and the worst in a person. Learning to be more disidentified helps a lot in clearing out misunderstandings. See the challenges as ways to learn and grow, and mainly, as you do this, remember to be in your heart, to listen to your heart, and to give energy from your heart.

Part Three: The Heart and the Higher Self

11

Using Heart Energy to Connect With the Higher Self

The best way to access the Higher Self is through the heart, as it is a direct link to this higher part of you. The Higher Self is the part within you that not only knows your potential but can also advise you on how to develop that potential. Everyone has special attributes that he is born with but does not necessarily know about. The Higher Self can reveal what is hidden and help the individual to acknowledge and work with it.

For example, you may have a desire to paint but have never taken a lesson. Suddenly, you feel the desire to do so. This inner desire is being prompted by the Higher Self, which knows that you have a hidden talent as a painter and this talent needs to be awakened.

Also, using the Higher Self to check situations and specific knowledge can be invaluable.

Your Higher Self can show you ways to develop other aspects of your personality, such as opening the heart, the ability to deeply listen to others, and enhancing your intuition and creativity. It is most definitely the part in you that is spiritual and connected to what are called Higher Sources. Most people think of the Higher Self as the wise part of themselves. It is the part that can bring someone knowledge and wisdom from Higher Sources.

Take time now to review the Higher Self exercises again at the back of this book and try doing the one that appeals to you the most. Remember, as stated in the beginning of the exercises section, it is very important to imagine sunlight shining down on the Higher Self and to see if the Self remains the same or becomes brighter. Often your desires can distort what you see, which is why when you shine light on what you perceive as your Higher Self, the image can disappear or get dark. Shining light is also a safeguard in case an imposter comes in and beguiles you. More is explained in the Higher Self exercises section.

The Higher Self is also the part in you that can truly help you psychologically. It has full understanding of your life and what has happened to you since you were born. Because it is so closely aligned with you, it can give you insights into things you have little understanding of: insights that can help you grow both psychologically and spiritually. When I say spiritually, I am not talking about a religion but about the characteristics of someone who has spiritual qualities, such as helping others, having compassion, loving others, and striving toward God Consciousness or the Source—qualities that are also of service in the world.

When you begin the practice of working with your Higher Self, you may find yourself becoming interested in world conditions and governmental policies as well as local community politics. Working with your Higher Self will expand your worldview and help you become more disidentified from emotions and what affects you. Remember, the Higher Self has no emotions, nor does it form any opinions; it simply looks at what is best and suggests actions following its truth. In other words, it always gives you the right advice for your personal growth. And it most definitely will help guide you in developing your heart.

Exercise:

>*Link with your Higher Self by doing one of the Higher Self exercises, and when you feel connected through the heart, ask the Higher Self the following questions:*
>*How can I use my heart's energy to connect with you? Give me a first step and then a process.*
>*When I am connected with you, how can I be more aware of what your advice is?*
>*Do I have any blocks to connecting with you?*
>*If the answer is yes, ask: How can I best remove those blocks?*
>*When I am truly connected with you, is there a specific feeling I will have?*

If the answer is yes, ask: What is the feeling?
Can you show me a specific image or symbol that best
represents you?
How should I use this image?
Basically, is there any advice you have for me that I
need to follow?
Is there anything stopping me from following your ad-
vice?

In doing this exercise, every time you ask a question, first shine sunlight down on the Higher Self. Even if you just feel energy in your heart that represents the Higher Self, still imagine the sunlight shining down on the energy. If the Higher Self is no longer there, you will feel the energy leave.

When you start working with your heart energy to connect with the Higher Self, you should feel a strong energy of warmth, expansion or movement enter your heart center. If you don't feel this, you are not fully connected with the Higher Self. You need to do the Higher Self exercise again, and when you feel connected, ask why you are having difficulty connecting to it with your heart.

Placing the symbol of the Higher Self that you were given in the above exercise in your heart should help you connect your heart energy with the Higher Self. It is also very helpful to draw your symbol and keep it on your desk or in another place where you will see it to remind yourself to link with the Higher Self during the day. Just linking with your heart brings in your Higher Self, and even if you aren't experiencing it consciously, it is still operating.

At the end of each day, go back over the events of that day and check whether or not you linked with your heart and your Higher Self. The more awareness you have of this action, the more it will help you on a daily basis. In the morning, link with your heart and ask that you remember to be in your heart throughout the day. This practice will become part of a daily routine that enhances your work and your relationships.

Here is an inspirational story about a young child named Stephan.

> He was eight years old and lived with his parents
> in a small country town. When he went to school
> each morning, he rode on a school bus, and then he
> returned home each afternoon on the bus. One morn-
> ing, the school bus never came, so he stayed home. His
> parents had already left for work, so he found himself

alone in the house for the first time. Stephan was a very precocious child, so he started to read a book that his mother was reading. The book was called Higher Self Yoga, and although it was an adult book, Stephan was able to read it.

In the beginning of the book was a Higher Self exercise, which he decided to try. It was the exercise of going up the mountain. At the top, when he asked that a figure come down from the sun, he saw a man dressed in a white robe with white hair and a white beard. He was fascinated, and at first did not know what to say or what to do. The man smiled at him and said, "Just link your heart to mine and experience how I feel."

"How do I do that?" Stephan replied.

"You first take your attention to the middle of your chest and ask that your heart link with my heart."

Stephan tried this, and when he linked with the Higher Self, he felt a great deal of warmth, and then he felt sadness come in, very intense sadness.

"I felt your great warmth, which was wonderful, but now I feel a lot of sadness. Why do I feel this way?"

"You are feeling what your mother is now feeling because you are very close to her and can pick up her feelings."

"But why is she so sad? I don't understand."

"Her sadness is because she is at the doctor's office right now. She was going to have a baby and has unfortunately just lost it."

"I didn't know I was going to have a brother or sister. How sad. I would have liked that."

"She hadn't told you yet because it was only a month old, and this has happened a couple of times before."

"Is there anything I can do?"

"Yes, when she comes home, tell her what has happened and tell her that she will become pregnant again and this time she will have the child, a beautiful girl."

"Oh, how wonderful! I've always wanted a sister. Thank you. I will tell her. Thank you."

"One more thing. Try to do this exercise again and come with a question you need me to answer, and make it a question about yourself that you need help with. I can help you with your schoolwork and your friendships. I am part of you, remember that." And the Higher Self faded from Stephan's vision.

When his mother came home in the afternoon, he told her the whole story. She started crying and hugged and hugged him. "I have tried several times to do that exercise, but without any luck, and you, my child, did it successfully. How wonderful! You are very special. As the book says, it takes a lot of practice to have results."

"He said to come and see Him with anything I need help with," said Stephan. "It was awesome, Mom, really awesome."

From then on, Stephan and his mother did the exercise together and read the book together. She would explain some of the things in the book that Stephan couldn't understand. She also was successful in seeing her Higher Self, and she was able to again become pregnant and did deliver a beautiful baby girl.

Stephan obviously was a special boy, who matured into a spiritual man. He constantly worked with his Higher Self and learned a great deal from it. This story shows the kind of knowledge that can come when you work with your heart and the Higher Self.

Exercise:

> *Ask your Higher Self the following questions:*
> *When I link my heart with you, can I experience your energy and also experience if someone I love is having problems?*
> *If the answer is no, ask: Why not?*
> *If I can experience someone having problems, how will I know the best way to help him?*
> *When I experience this, will I feel it in my heart or just know it in my mind?*

113

If I experience it in my mind, would it be better to feel it in my heart?

Some people will just know something in the mind and that is fine. It's not always necessary to experience it in the heart. The main thing is to realize the best way to use the information. Sometimes you can be sent information from the Higher Self through the mind, and then you can put that information into your heart and ask what the best way would be to handle it. Sometimes you only need to know something and act on it, and other times you need to be more involved in a manner that is not imposing.

With most people, it's always important to ask if they want help before giving it. The only exceptions are those people who don't have all their mental faculties or small children. But if a child is over the age of six, then you also need to ask him. Some children are very independent and want to try to do something on their own and don't want anyone to help them.

Recently, a friend's child, who was seven years old, needed help pinning a piece of art on the wall of his room. His father tried to do it for him, but the child didn't want the help, even though he couldn't reach the place he wanted to put the art. So his father got a small stepladder and held it for him so he could go up and pin his piece of art. That was a sound way to solve the problem. If the father had insisted on doing it, his son would no longer have liked the art. Using the heart means understanding the best way to solve a problem.

Exercise:

Do the Higher Self exercise of your choice, and ask your Higher Self the following questions:
If I am trying to help someone, what is the best way for me to approach the person?
If the person says no, do I say anything in return?
If I know someone is going to try to do something that I feel may harm him, how do I handle that situation?

If you can see that a situation is overkill yet the person is insistent on doing the task, it's important, then, to stand by and help him in the work whether he wants you there or not. When he sees it's too much for him, then he can use your help.

If you know someone needs help and you are unable to help him, it's important to find someone who can step in and do that. This happens frequently when a person is older and not able to function as well as he used to. Perhaps someone you know is stronger and younger and would be willing to help, or if you can't find someone like that, you could try to hire someone to come in and do the work. Offering to pay someone is another form of help.

Too many people will try to do an impossible task and never think of asking for help. This can prove difficult, and often dangerous.

Exercise:

> *Ask yourself the following questions:*
> *Do I ask for help when I need it?*
> *If the answer is no, ask: Why not?*
> *Do I feel that if I ask for help, I need to either pay the person or return the favor some day?*
> *If the answer is yes, ask: Why do I feel this way?*
> *Do I in any way feel embarrassed if I cannot do something myself?*
> *If the answer is yes, ask: Why?*
> *If I have help in doing something, do I feel genuinely grateful?*
> *If the answer is no, ask: Why not?*

Sometimes, having a favor given to you is something you really do not want. Ask your Higher Self the following questions:

> *What is the best way for me to refuse without hurting the person's feelings?*
> *When I say no, do I really mean it, or do I in any way want to be persuaded?*
> *When someone does something for me, can I accept that with gratitude and without feelings of regret about letting myself be helped?*
> *If the answer is no, ask: Why not?*

It's difficult when a person has always been able to do things on his own and then something happens and he has to be helped. If this is something that has happened to you, ask your Higher Self the following questions:

> *How can I accept that I need help at this time?*
> *Can I accept help without feeling bad that I can't do something myself?*
> *If the answer is no, ask: How do I change this feeling?*

A friend's mother grew old and had a difficult time accepting that she could no longer do things on her own. When my friend would go and do things for her, she often tried to pay him, and when he refused to take anything, it would make her upset. He saw this and it really bothered him. He told her he was only doing a little in return for all the help she had given him for years. But she had a difficult time accepting this. Finally, he told her to bake him some of the cookies he loved so much. She happily did this and felt much better. He would take the cookies home and give them away, but letting her do this little thing made a big difference in her being able to ask for help when she needed it.

Some people need to do something in return, so accepting something little like this helps them. Others will buy gifts for you, and that's all right too, but never expect to receive anything for help given. It's given from the heart and that is enough. Using your heart energy to help someone is always in itself a great reward because it opens your heart and helps you grow spiritually.

Heart energy is a wonderful gift to give someone.

Someone asked the Dalai Lama, "India is full of poverty. What can we do to help these people when there isn't enough money to give out?"

His reply was, "Of course it is impossible for you to give money to feed all the poor people on the streets, but you can send the beggar love from your heart. That will feed his soul."

12

Using Heart Energy to Connect to One's Spiritual Path

A spiritual path needs to be felt in the heart. Whether you go to church or are involved in an esoteric teaching, you need a heart commitment to follow the path; otherwise, you just practice it one day a week and don't think about it the rest of the week. If you have a heart commitment, it means you either pray or meditate on a daily basis. You also think about and sometimes read from the scriptures you are following, and this also is a daily practice. In other words, your heart links to this practice whether it involves a western religion, such as Judaism or Christianity, or an eastern religion such as Islam, Buddhism or any style of Yoga. In all religions there is an esoteric version that is followed by a smaller group of believers.

There are also many people who do not follow any religious practice but consider themselves agnostics or atheists. If you are either of these, then this chapter may not interest you, but you may want to look at it. For everyone else, try doing the exercises, as they will help you to feel a deeper commitment to whatever path you follow.

What is a spiritual path? It can be defined as any practice a person follows that makes her feel closer to what, in western society, is called God or God Consciousness. It is a practice that is meaningful to a person's life, something that is practiced in the heart daily. It can be followed in any place. It's not necessary to go to a church, or synagogue, or any institution, but can simply be practiced in one's home and even with one's family.

A common routine would be blessing the food you eat, or even saying blessings over the food while you are cooking. It can be saying a prayer when you go to sleep, or meditating on a daily basis. Devotional practice can consist of sending love to a Divine Being of any faith. Devotion of any kind is having an open heart and using the heart's energy in a positive manner. When you open your heart, the energy can be very strong and it can be used to help the planet (see Chapter 26).

A friend of mine always meditates in the early morning before going to work. During his meditations, he began to see another man, whom he didn't know, sitting and meditating. They would nod to each other and both continue to meditate. This went on for a few years, until one day my friend went on a job interview with the president of a large corporation. My friend was startled when he met him, because the man was the same man he had been seeing for years. They both smiled in recognition, and for the first time, exchanged names and discussed their respective meditation practices. This company was in another city, where my friend was thinking of moving. The only thing both had in common was that they meditated every day at the same time.

Heart energy can be sent out, and it also can attract spiritual things to you. If, for example, you are praying for someone, you are open to receiving someone else's heart energy being sent to you. This happens frequently, especially with loved ones. If you also believe in a Higher spiritual Being, such as Jesus, Buddha or Mohammad, sending love and devotion to that Being opens your heart to receiving a similar energy from that Being. People who have deep devotion may sometimes receive a vision of the Being they are devoted to while they are praying or meditating. This vision can penetrate the heart and open it more fully.

Try looking at a picture of someone you feel devotion for. Just look at the face and try focusing on it for five minutes without any thoughts coming in. Next, close your eyes and try to see the same picture in your mind's eye. Hold that image and send your heart energy to it. The more you do this, the easier it becomes to remember the image so that you can carry it in your heart at all times. This links your heart to that individual and strengthens the love and devotion.

The Higher Self is also the part in you that helps you on your spiritual path. It will help guide you in your spiritual practice and can bring you higher wisdom from Higher Beings. It is your link to the higher realms.

Exercise:

Ask your Higher Self the following questions, adding the name of the Higher Being you feel closest to:
When I link my heart with _____, what should I be feeling?
Is there any way in which I can have a vision of _____ ?
How can I develop my devotion to _____?
How can I remember to link with _____ on a daily basis?
What else should I know in terms of my connection with _____ ?

In the eastern religions, practitioners use strings of prayer beads called malas. In Catholicism, prayer beads are used in meditation and in praying to the Virgin Mary. It may benefit you to buy some prayer beads and recite the name of the Higher Being with each bead. In the East, the prayer is *Jai* followed by the name of the Higher Being. Jai is a form of praise. You can do this or just say *Praise be to* _____. The rhythm of doing this helps to deepen the devotion and also helps to bring the individual closer to the chosen image.

There is a story about an East Indian man named Ananda, who studied yoga with a very well-known guru who lived in the south of India. His ashram was very large and housed not only the devotees who lived there, but also had room for the frequent visitors who would come for a short time to study the teaching.

Ananda was one of these visitors. He had come from the north of India to study for three months. His family, consisting of his wife and two children, had wanted to come with him, but some family problems arose which kept them at home. His wife prayed every day for his safe return and for his spiritual progress. Her heart energy was very strong, and he could feel her there with him even when the guru was teaching. It was as if she had come with him.

One day during meditation, he saw her clearly and she looked very sad. He asked her, "Why are you sad? Did something happen?"

She answered, "Yes, our son Madhu had an accident and has died," and she started to cry in the vision.

Ananda told his teacher what had happened and the teacher said he would help Madhu on the other side. He closed his eyes and did this. When he opened his eyes again, he said to Ananda, "Your son would like to say goodbye to you."

"How can I do that?"

"Go back to meditating and I will take you to him."

Ananda did this and felt his teacher take him somewhere, and there he saw a vision of his son. He embraced him and said goodbye and that he hoped to see him again in another life.

Madhu said he felt very happy, but that he was concerned about his mother. He said she was weeping all the time for him, and this was holding him back so he couldn't continue on.

Ananda said he would tell her not to do this.

When he meditated again, he called to his wife and finally saw her. He told her what Madhu had said and that she needed to stop her sorrow and let him go on. She said she would try.

Ananda asked his guru if he should go home to be with her.

"But she is here all the time with you, surely you know this?"

"Yes, but maybe she needs me physically to be there."

"No, she needs you more to be with her spiritually at this time."

So Ananda stayed the full three months, and when he returned, he embraced his wife and told her all that had happened. She then told him that she had been fully aware of what had transpired, and that she had attended every class with him. She missed her son but knew it was right to stop the mourning process so he could go on.

This story shows how strong the heart energy is, and that when there is strong devotion and love, it's possible to do miraculous things. Ananda's wife had such devotion to the guru and such love for her husband that the energy brought her to be with them both. It was just as surprising for her as it was for Ananda. They both had taken extensive notes of the teaching, and comparing their notes, verified that she indeed had been there for every class. Of course, the guru's energy helped make this happen also.

Using the heart's energy spiritually brings you a deeper understanding of your own spiritual nature. When this happens, you will feel the true meaning of having heart energy, as it is completely connected to spiritual energy. Spiritual energy comes through the heart, and when you have it, you feel the deeper meaning of devotional practice. Some people who have a strong spiritual nature feel this automatically, but others may have spiritual convictions that are more in the nature of beliefs formed by the mind. Taking those beliefs and putting them into your heart will give a deeper meaning to them.

For example, you may have a belief in a Supreme Being of some kind, but not necessarily a man beaming down from heaven. You can take that belief in a Supreme Being and simply place it into your heart and ask to feel in your heart that there is a Supreme Being of some kind that began our world. You may then feel warmth in your heart or energy, or you may feel nothing. In the first instance, your heart is confirming that this belief is true for you. In the second case, if you feel nothing, your heart is confirming that you may think this on some level, but you don't really believe it.

Exercise:

> *Write down some of your spiritual beliefs, and then,*
> *one at a time, put each belief into your heart and hold*
> *it there. Write down the responsive feeling, or the lack*
> *of feeling, that you have. Do this on different days for*
> *each belief; don't do one after another. The heart needs*
> *to clear out the energy of each one, and that may take a*
> *few hours.*
> *If you find that you have no response in your heart, ask*
> *your Higher Self: How did I arrive at this belief?*

The belief could be coming from your childhood family beliefs, or even from close friends.

If you have no belief in a Supreme Being, put this into your heart by saying, "May my heart feel if I truly do believe in a Supreme Being." If you have a strong feeling, that means you really do believe in such a Being, but if your heart doesn't respond, this signifies you really don't feel the statement is correct. If that is the case, ask your Higher Self, "Why don't I believe in a Supreme Being?" Lack of belief can come from the mind and intellectual thinking, or even from friends and family who are very analytical.

If this is the case, try experiencing what it would feel like to believe in something that started it all. Put the question into your heart, "How would it feel to believe in something Higher that brought about the universe and all that is part of it?"

A spiritual path may be an active one where you consciously study a certain teaching, or it may be one where you simply have beliefs but never take them into an active program of development. In both paths, the heart energy plays a certain role. Without this energy, beliefs will remain dormant and you will have a difficult time on any path that you follow. Try using your heart daily in any practice you follow and soon you will feel comfortable, and no longer vulnerable, using it for all your activities.

Without the heart energy, a person would have a passive personality and live a life that lacks love, adventure, hope, and positive energy. Most of all, that life would lack any spiritual commitment.

13

Using the Heart With the Higher Self to Look at Characteristics

The heart and the Higher Self work very closely together, even when you least realize it. Mainly, they control the higher feelings as well as the mechanisms for inner spiritual and mental growth.

When the Higher Self is fully operating in an individual, the person is literally achieving his full potential. This is because the Higher Self is regulated by the positive patterns that are within each person. You may wonder how this works. If you believe in karma and that you came into this life with karmic patterns, some of which are negative and need to be experienced and changed, and some of which are positive and need to be developed, then you will understand how these play out in your life.

If you don't believe in karma, then you may believe that there are definite characteristics that come genetically through your family and those characteristics constitute who you are.

In both cases, you believe you have within you a higher nature and a lower nature. In the first case, you would believe that the higher nature and the lower nature are developed through many lifetimes. In the second case, you may believe that the higher nature and the lower nature come from your family.

Most of you do have a belief that something in you operates from a good place and that there is another part of you that operates from a negative place.

If you want to improve yourself and get rid of some of your negative characteristics, your Higher Self, or higher nature, can help you do this. For example, you may have a tendency to be argumentative. You can ask your Higher Self to help you stop doing this.

Exercise:

> *Write a list of the negative characteristics you know you have and that you really would like to rid yourself of. Examples might be:*
> - *Competitive*
> - *Jealous*
> - *Critical*
> - *Manipulative*
> - *Aggressive*
> - *Controlling*
> - *Egotistical*
> - *Manipulating*
> - *Demanding*
> - *Pleaser*
>
> *You may have other negative characteristics that you want to add to your list.*
>
> *After you have the list, prioritize it, putting the worst one at the top. Taking the top one, link with your Higher Self and ask the following questions:*
> *When did this characteristic come into being?*
> *Is it from my family conditioning?*
> *Is it from a past life?*
> *Is it something that I really would like to change?*
> *If the answer is yes, then ask: What would be a good process and a first step in changing it?*
> *If the answer is no, then ask: Why not?*

When you start to work with these negative aspects, do so slowly, and try doing a nightly review at the end of the day, going back over the day and recognizing when that characteristic came up. Notice if the characteristic comes out with certain people, and also if it comes out in certain circumstances.

In the morning, remind yourself to be aware of when you get into this characteristic, and try changing it at the moment it occurs.

Sometimes you can be in a negative place and not really be aware you are in it. The next time you are conscious of feeling negative, try to simply step back from the feeling, look at it, and ask yourself how this happened. If you are aware of the stepping-stones that take you there, then you can stop the process before it reaches the final point of being fully in the characteristic. It takes constant effort to be fully aware, but when you start to realize how a negative characteristic is triggered, it is easier to stop the process.

Sometimes a negative characteristic gives you something that you want to hold on to, and because of this 'payoff' you don't want to give the characteristic up.

For instance, if you are argumentative and always win arguments, that may give you a sense of power over someone, particularly if this is a common occurrence with a specific person. You may win because the person backs down when he hears your tone of voice. If you simply discuss something and disagree, this would not necessarily make a person back down; but an argumentative tone of voice can be very authoritarian, and this may cause a person to give up rather than pursue the discussion. This may happen with a certain person only. You then need to look deep within and ask yourself why you need to overpower this person. It may not be a characteristic that you use with anyone else. If this is the case, I would suggest that you do the following exercise:

Exercise:

> *Ask your Higher Self the following questions:*
> *Why do I always get into this behavior with this person?*
> *Also ask: Is there some past history with this person*
> *that makes this behavior of mine happen with him?*
> *Then ask: How can I change this behavior and not continue this pattern?*

Now look back at your list, and next to each negative characteristic, write down the names of anyone with whom you get into the characteristic and behavior. Then, go through the above questions for each characteristic and person. When you plan to have a meeting with one of the people, look back at this exercise and the answers your Higher Self gave you about the characteristic. Try to avoid getting into the pattern, and notice how it feels to be more congenial. Also notice if there is a change in behavior from the person.

Often, negative characteristics are acquired over a long period of time and become automatic when you are in the presence of someone you have conflicts with. Or, you could have acquired a negative characteristic from watching others in your childhood. It's good to change the pattern and notice how that changes the outcome.

Here is a story that illustrates this:

> In a country far away in the eastern part of the world, there were mostly men and very few females because of the difficult mountainous terrain and the cold climate.
>
> In a certain village lived a young man who was a sturdy hard worker. His name was Klahan, and he had been born and raised in the village and had never ventured forth to more cosmopolitan places. There were many men in his village, and just a few of them were married. The rest were bachelors or too young to settle down. All the men worked in a mine in the mountain, mining iron ore.
>
> The village was in an isolated valley in the mountains; in the wintertime it was completely snowed in, with no access to the towns bordering the mountain. Because of this, most of the food supplies had to be brought up in the spring and summer and stored in cool places dug into the mountain. It was a hard and sometimes dangerous life for everyone. A medicine man was the only medical person there to care for the sick and injured, but he didn't have good skills. The nearest hospital was at the foot of the mountain many miles below. Generally, when someone became ill or was injured, he would die and his body was burned. The life expectancy was low; some would live to forty or fifty, but that was rare.
>
> At the time this story takes place, it was spring, and Klahan was in his late twenties. He had never mar-

ried and wanted to find someone to have a family with. His father had raised him because his mother had died in childbirth when Klahan was small, so he had very little experience in how to talk and be with a woman. His father was rough and coarse and raised his son to be the same.

The few times that Klahan went into the village proper, he looked at the girls but was afraid to talk with any of them. When he tried, his mannerisms were bold and impolite. He was sexually attracted to every girl he met. Like a dog in heat, he would even try to grab them and kiss them without considering whether they wanted him to do so or not.

The few times he finally ventured further down into the nearest town, his mannerisms and behavior were the same. Almost immediately, as soon as he was spotted by someone in the town, the single women would hide in their houses until he left. It was a shame, because Klahan was essentially a warm-hearted man, very attractive, and a good worker who had some nice qualities to offer a woman.

He had a good friend, Sunan, whom he asked for advice. His friend told him truthfully that no woman would want to marry him when he talked in a coarse manner, and also that he was too grabby. Sunan explained that women had to be treated differently, more gently and with patience. He had to learn how to listen and communicate in a way that would attract a woman to him.

So Klahan tried to do this. He tried and tried and tried, and each time it seemed a woman was listening to him, he would make an unsavory remark that would turn her off. Sunan would listen to what happened and explain to him what went wrong, but Klahan's conditioning was such that he always bungled it.

Sunan was married to a lovely woman, and they lived part-time in the town and part-time in the mountain village. This was because she wanted to raise their children in a more cultured place, where there were better schools and a chance for them to do other kinds of work.

Sunan himself wanted to leave the mountain village and the mining, but it was the only work he had ever done, so he needed to develop other skills. He was beginning to do so in the town when he was there part time, but this meant that he only worked part time, which gave them little money to live on.

One day when he was talking to Klahan, who was in a very depressed state, he came up with an idea. "Why don't you come live with Kulap and me in town? Kulap can help you change your behavior with women and may even have an idea about who would be a good wife for you. You can pay us for room and board and that would help us financially while I go to school here."

Klahan liked the idea, as he had saved a lot of money hoping to buy a house and settle down. Kulap didn't like the idea very much, as she never liked the way Klahan behaved in general and certainly could understand why women ran from him even though he was very handsome. But she finally agreed, as they did need some financial help.

Klahan decided to stay there through the summer, taking leave from his mining job. The first plan was for Klahan to just observe the way in which Kulap and Sunan conversed. He was not to speak to Kulap at all for at least three weeks, but just listen and watch them together. When he didn't understand something, he could ask why they acted or spoke in that manner.

It was an interesting experience for him. At first it was difficult for him to understand when Sunan was affectionate with her. He would hug her and touch her gently. Finally, Klahan asked, "I don't understand why you don't grab her ass. She's your wife. I would think that would be okay to do."

Kulap explained that in general women don't like to be grabbed, even by their husbands. It might be all right to do in certain circumstances, but not in front of other people. That was considered rude.

When Klahan observed Sunan and Kulap talking, he noticed that they spoke in a soft, loving way. He asked, "Does love make you talk to each other in such a manner?"

"Yes, there is love, but we mainly use our hearts when we talk and try not to be in our minds," said Kulap. "When we do this with each other, it also gives us the ability to be in our hearts when we talk with others. Do you feel that coming from us when we talk with you?"

"Yes, I have felt it, but I thought it was a friendship way of talking."

"It is that also, but even with strangers you can use your heart."

After several weeks of such learning, Kulap started to have conversations with Klahan. When his replies were off, she would correct him and tell him a better way to say what he wanted to express. All this was learning totally new behavior for him, but as he grew confident he became better at it.

Finally, Kulap sat down with him and said, "It's time for you to meet some women. There is going to be a dance this weekend and I think you should go, but you will need to learn quickly how to dance."

This was another thing Klahan had never learned, so, patiently, Kulap practiced with him every day until he could lead and follow the music.

It was summer now and the night of the dance was warm and clear, with stars shining in the cloudless sky. With Sunan's help, Klahan had bought some new clothes for the occasion.

The dance was being held outdoors, with lanterns strung around an open area. When Klahan first arrived, the women clustered together and walked to the other side. But they watched as Kulap put her arm through his and they chatted amiably. Then he danced with her and did not seem aggressive. After the dance,

Sunan joined them and they went to get some refreshments. Kulap, at that point, started talking with some people she knew.

She came back to Klahan and said, "It's time to meet the ladies. Remember to be in your heart."

She brought him over to the ladies and reintroduced him, as he had met many of them before. One woman was very pretty, and she gave him a little curtsy. He returned it with a bow and she giggled. He danced with her and chatted, and then he danced with another lady, who was quite chic in a long white dress and with flowers in her hair.

From then on, things changed. Klahan was dating and developing relationships with a couple of the women. His mannerisms were always perfect, and when he wasn't certain how to respond, he didn't say anything and later checked it out with Kulap or Sunan.

There was one woman in particular whom he started to care about. Her name was Lawan. She lived with her father, who had a shop in town. Lawan was well educated and helped her father with the business, but she also made it clear that she did not want to ever live in the village on the mountain. She had visited there once with her father and hated the ugliness of the place and the rough living.

Klahan had never thought about leaving home, but when confronted with the dilemma of losing Lawan, he decided to develop a business himself in the village. He offered to help her father expand his store, adding tradesman's wear and equipment that he knew was needed back in his village and possibly in other hill towns and villages as well.

Her father agreed to the plan, and also to Klahan and Lawan getting married, and Klahan soon became a prosperous businessman, returning home on occasion to sell supplies to his friends there.

It was a whole life change for Klahan, but the major change was confronting his negative characteristics and changing them. His desire to marry was strong enough for him to really do the hard work of overcoming patterns he had carried from childhood.

This chapter has talked about looking at negative characteristics and changing them with the help of the heart and the Higher Self.

It's also good to acknowledge and look at your positive characteristics, with the desire to enhance them and make them a fuller part of your daily life. People have positive aspects that they often neglect to nurture and truly realize. These aspects not only can help you in the work you do, but they certainly will help you in all your relationships. Knowing that they exist but not working to make them even better can cause them to become dormant. It's good to start by recognizing what they are.

Here are examples of positive qualities:

- Intuitive
- Compassionate
- Nurturing
- Responsive
- Patient
- Creative
- Assertive
- Courageous
- Generous
- Focused

You may have other positive characteristics that you want to add to your list.

Exercise:

> *Make a list of all the positive characteristics or qualities that you believe you have. Rate them one to ten in terms of how much you use them daily, ten signifying a quality you use a lot.*
> *Then, check the list and the ratings with your Higher Self. Also, ask if there is a quality that you forgot to put down.*
> *Taking the lowest rated one, ask your Higher Self:*

How can I use this quality more in my daily life?
Is there anything that is preventing me from using it?
If the answer is yes, ask: What is it, and how can I
change it?
If the answer is no, ask: Is there any other reason why I
am not using this quality more?
If the answer is yes, ask: What is it?
When I use this quality, how can I best acknowledge
that I am using it?
Is there anything I need to do to develop it more fully?
Is this quality something I developed in this life, or was
I born with it?

After you have worked with enhancing this quality and feel it is a part of your daily routine, take the next quality and work with that. Start by asking the Higher Self the above questions.

As you work with the next quality, check if you have forgotten the first quality you were enhancing. Sometimes when someone goes on to another quality, he forgets the first one and it falls back to where it was before.

Using your heart and Higher Self to work with negative and positive qualities is very important in your life and in your relationships. Don't feel discouraged if it takes time to do. The main thing to remember is that enhancement of the positive and reduction of the negative will make a big difference in your life, and it will also help you to continue developing the energy of your heart.

14

Using the Heart with the Higher Self to Refine One's Personality

Your heart is the main center that helps you in your personal growth. Using your heart is a way you can start to see yourself more clearly. So often a person has no clear understanding of how she appears to others, nor does she have any idea how she sounds to others. Personality also varies according to whom you are speaking with. For example, if you are having a conversation with someone you love, you will speak in a warm manner. If you are instead talking to a stranger, your voice may be without any emotion. Your voice can change if you are feeling any negative emotions toward someone. Because of this, you are not always conscious of how you sound to someone. Also, if you are in a negative mood, you can project that mood in your voice even when talking with a loved one.

It is important to be fully conscious of how you sound, mainly because the voice carries emotions that can bring about a positive or negative response from the person with whom you are speaking. For example, if you have a strong authoritative background from your childhood, you could have taken on some of that characteristic in the manner in which you speak. You may have no awareness that you sound that way and may be surprised if you are accused of being too authoritarian. If you believe in past lives, you may also realize that some of these mannerisms could be brought over from a past life.

The following is a list of mannerisms that you could demonstrate and which you may or may not be aware of:

- Speaking in a harsh manner.

- Speaking in an authoritarian manner.

- Speaking in a soft and sometimes inaudible manner.

- Speaking in a forceful and domineering manner.

- Slurring your words.

- Speaking too quickly, so it's difficult to follow what you are saying.

- Speaking in a way that is so loud it disturbs others around you.

- Interrupting.

- Not looking at the person you are talking to.

- Having a lot of interjections in your speech such as "hmm," or "you know," or clearing your throat.

- Not articulating when you talk, so people can't understand what you are talking about.

- Being self-conscious when you talk, showing nervousness.

These are just some of the modes of speaking that are difficult to listen to.

Exercise:

> *Link with your heart and your Higher Self and go over the above list. With each item, ask yourself if you speak in such a manner, marking clearly those items for which you have a yes. Prioritize your list; then, focusing first on the one you do most often, ask your Higher Self the following questions:*
> *Is there a reason why I speak this way?*
> *Did I do this in my childhood?*
> *Does it relate to a past life? Or, to a family characteristic I was not aware of?*

> *How can I best change my pattern? Give me a process*
> *and a first step.*

When you start to work with these speech patterns, don't try to work with all of them at once. It's important to focus on just one at a time. Work on this with a nightly review in which you ask yourself, "Did I speak in this manner with anyone today?" Notice if you fall into the pattern with a particular person. If that is true, try to be careful when you are with that person. Always link with your heart and ask to speak in a very neutral manner when you are with her.

It's important to always speak in a neutral or loving manner with everyone. If you are feeling some strong emotions toward someone, what can help is giving those emotions to your Higher Self. Try the following exercise:

Exercise:

> *Link with your heart. Then, imagine that you have a*
> *black garbage bag and you can easily take any negative*
> *feelings you have toward the person you will be meet-*
> *ing out of your heart. Imagine these feelings as black*
> *blotches and put them into the garbage bag. When you*
> *feel free of all of them, hand the bag to your Higher Self,*
> *saying, "Please take these from me temporarily, so I can*
> *speak with this person in a neutral manner."*
> *Obviously, if you are holding onto such feelings, you*
> *need to try to understand them, and perhaps at a later*
> *time also heal those feelings by talking with the person.*
> *Then it is even more important to do this exercise so*
> *that your conversation won't be aggressive or too con-*
> *frontational.*

The manner in which we speak is one of the ways we display attitudes and feelings. Correcting emotions is very important in relating to others. The heart and Higher Self can help you do this. Some people are much more emotional than others, and this applies to both men and women. There is nothing wrong with having emotional feelings, as long as they don't become overly pronounced and you are aware that you are demonstrating them. There is nothing worse than hearing someone who is angry and yelling, or someone who is overly dramatizing a situation. Any uncontrolled behavior is a problem for anyone to listen to. If someone is constantly doing this, others will not want to be with that person.

The following is a list of some difficult behaviors:

- Being argumentative.
- Yelling or screaming at someone.
- Crying or overly dramatizing a situation.
- Acting out with bodily movements.
- Looking and acting disgusted about something.
- Appearing under the influence of a substance.
- Laughing to an extreme.
- Doing something outlandish for attention.
- Being moody and withdrawn.
- Putting someone down.
- Being sarcastic.
- Having to always take charge of any situation.
- Having to be the center of attention.

Exercise:

Go over the list and pick out the behaviors you feel you may do. Check with your Higher Self to verify your list, and then prioritize it, with the one you do the most at the top. Then, starting with the top item, ask your Higher Self the following questions about each behavior: Why do I act this way at times?

Is there a specific person or situation that causes me to act this way?

Did I do this in my childhood?

If the answer is yes, ask: What were the reactions of the people around me?

Am I always aware that I am doing this?

If the answer is no, ask: How can I become more aware?

If the answer is yes, ask: Do I ever try to change this at the time?

*Is this mannerism something that I want to hold on to
because it gives me something?*
*If the answer is yes, ask: What does it give me, and how
can I let go of that?*
*How can I best start to change this behavior? Give me a
first step.*

Then continue the process by working with the other items in the same way.

The following is a story that illustrates bad behavior:

> A man called Thomas lived in a big city in a very small, rent-controlled apartment. He was in his fifties and did fundraising for a not-for-profit organization. He had never been married and had very few friends, mainly because his personality was so negative. He constantly yelled at his fellow workers, to the point that no one liked to deal with him. He kept his job mainly because his work was good. Even though his boss asked him to be less argumentative, Thomas couldn't control his temper. He yelled that the work handed to him was flawed and not good enough. He yelled at just about anything he couldn't control.
>
> A woman named Nancy came to work there. She was in charge of a department that had to deal directly with him. She was a fine worker and was liked by her new co-workers and staff. Thomas almost immediately found fault with her work and complained about it to his superior, who fortunately never paid any attention to his outbursts. He started calling her about jobs and screaming at her over the phone. He even called her one time and told her that he was going to get her fired.
>
> At first she hung up on him, and when she talked to her boss he explained that Thomas did this to everyone. He said that Thomas was a bit nuts, but since he had been there for twenty years, did a good job, and was in the union, they didn't have a strong case to fire him.

This kept bothering Nancy, so she spoke to a spiritual teacher she knew who gave her interesting advice, which she followed. The next time Thomas phoned and started his yelling routine, she laughed at him.

"Why are you laughing?" he asked, outraged.

"You're just so funny," she said.

And he hung up on her.

This happened a few times, and then he stopped yelling! In fact, he started their conversations with, "Hi sweetie, how is everything?" and she now responded sweetly. His staff started to notice his mannerism with her and asked her what had happened. How had she changed him? She told them the story and they all couldn't believe it.

In the meantime, Thomas kept up his yelling routine with the other staff members, until he became sick and found that he had an ulcer. His doctor told him he had to always remain calm and not get upset about anything. This made him change completely. He even started meeting people outside the office and making friends for the first time.

This solution was about using a reverse strategy, one method that can work when someone uses harsh mannerisms toward you or speaks in a way that you don't understand. Here is a summary of my suggestions:

If someone yells at you, just laugh, following Nancy's method.

Another way of dealing with screaming behavior is to start talking softly and always being calm; the more someone yells, the quieter you make your voice.

If neither of these work, simply say, "When you can speak like an adult and not like a child, I will talk with you," and leave or hang up.

If someone takes control over what you are doing, ask her in a calm voice what she thinks she is doing. If the answer is, "I'm fixing this," then answer, "I think what you are doing is not fixing it but hindering it. I would appreciate you fixing your own things, not mine."

Always smile and be calm, but direct. In other words, confronting what is going on is better than giving in to it. If the person is your boss, you can still question why she is taking over the work she has given you to do. If she doesn't like your work, ask her what she wants you to do. Keep it your job, not hers. If she wants you to do something that you think is wrong, then firmly disagree and ask her how what she wants would make it better.

If someone is aggressive and domineering, handle this behavior by reverse behavior. Never fight back; it will be a losing battle. Instead, do the soft speaking routine and pretend not to hear her. Start doing another task, or ask her if she wants some coffee or tea. Always ignore the behavior when it is overly strong. If she wants an answer, simply say, "You won't hear any answer I give."

It's fine to tell someone who is slurring her words, or talking too quickly, or too softy, "Please repeat what you just said, I didn't understand you." If you know the person well, you can mention to her what she is doing wrong, but always do this in a loving way.

Every interactive situation will bring out aspects of your personality. Mainly, it's important to try to be disidentified, as this will keep you calm and help you receive good advice from your Higher Self, which knows the best way to act or react. Awareness of what is taking place is also key whenever you are in a difficult situation. Remember to link with your heart and your Higher Self, and ask what is happening when things feel confusing and unclear or you are in doubt. Sometimes someone will enter a conversation and cause disturbances to occur. It is also good to know the best method of handling this.

Exercise:

> *Think back to a difficult situation where words were said, or not said, and the main feeling was one of discomfort. See and experience exactly what took place. Try to remember the exact words that were said and the emotions that came out... Now, relive the scene, but this time imagine you are looking down on it and watching your interaction and what happened. Notice if there is anything new you were not aware of before. Then link with your heart and ask your Higher Self:*
> *What was the cause of the discomfort?*
> *Could it in any way have been avoided?*
> *If the answer is yes, ask: How?*
> *How could I have changed what happened, or what did I need to say?*

Next, close your eyes and replay the scene, this time following the advice your Higher Self gave you. How does this feel? What changed? Was the outcome different?

In any given situation, events can change if you always stay in your heart. The heart, when linked to the Higher Self, understands the correct way to be. The more you practice being in your heart and linking to your Higher Self, the more you can change the negative aspects of your personality into positive ones.

15

The Battle Between the
Higher Self and the Lower Nature

When someone starts to work with the heart and links with the Higher Self, the energy that happens as a result of the interaction will open parts of the person that may have been dormant. These parts vary from spiritual feelings to lower nature feelings. Often as you work with the Higher Self, the lower self or lower nature becomes more active: for example, there may be repressed lower nature desires such as love of wealth, sexual desires, and other aspects of the personality that are negative. Some of these were explored in Chapter 13.

When these desires and other negative aspects suddenly become stronger, you can be certain that there is a battle taking place between your Higher Self, or higher nature, and your lower nature.

To define it better, the lower nature is that part in you that has negative characteristics and also magnified desires, whereas your higher nature contains all your positive characteristics, spiritual desires and higher emotions. The higher nature contains love and compassion, whereas the lower nature contains hatred and greed.

When this inner battle starts, you may suddenly have negative desires that you have never experienced before. These desires were always there, but you were either not aware of them, or you never listened to them because your higher nature was stronger. Now, the lower nature will become stronger in order for you to work with it more. Many Eastern teachings call the lower nature the 'dweller on the threshold' and the higher nature the Higher Self, that part in you that contains the seed of the spirit, or what you may call the God within. The story of Jesus being tempted by Satan in the wilderness is an example of this battle.

Someone on a spiritual quest will work with the higher nature and experience confrontations with personal demons in the lower nature. Here are some of the characteristics of the lower nature:

- Strong negative characteristics such as the need to control or dominate others.
- Strong emotions such as anger and lustfulness.
- Strong needs such as the need for wealth, mundane treasures of any kind, and also any addictions.
- Strong feelings of malice and deceitfulness, or wanting to manipulate someone.
- Competitiveness.
- Strong sexual desires that can be extreme and unbalanced.
- Fears that can overpower you.
- Negative thoughts about people, even loved ones.
- Strong feelings of mistrust, not based on reality.
- Greed.

These are just some examples of what your lower nature can contain, and some of these may not be visible or felt most of the time. If you believe in past lives, you may believe that characteristics from negative lives may emerge, some of which you have not experienced up to this point. The main thing to remember when this happens is that you also have a higher nature, which contains the pure and beautiful parts of who you are. It's important to not succumb to feelings of self-criticism or shame when the negative things start to be felt. Remember, every human contains both of these areas within. Everyone has done wrong and negative things throughout their evolution. Even if what comes up is totally new for you, it's important to not try to repress the feelings but rather to disidentify from them. Simply notice them and then discard them. Do not repress them; otherwise, they become hidden tendencies that can still be played out when you least expect it.

Exercise:

> *When you start to work with your heart and Higher Self, every evening go over the day and notice if something negative came up for you that day. Did you have negative thoughts? Did you feel negative feelings? Did you do something that was a little off, something you have never done before? Look at the day carefully, and make a list of things that were coming from your lower nature. Notice the 'story' around them. Did a particular person push your buttons or irritate you?*
>
> *Then, in the morning, ask to be more aware of when a negative tendency comes up during the day, and try to catch it.*

When you can do that, you can consciously change that thought or action to a positive one by linking with your heart and giving the negative characteristic to your Higher Self to eliminate, as described in the previous chapter.

Exercise:

> *Taking the list of lower nature tendencies that you made in the first exercise above, add any others you may believe you have. Then link with your heart and ask your Higher Self the following questions about each one:*
>
> *How strong is this tendency in me? Give it a number from one to ten, ten being the strongest.*
>
> *Did I develop this in my childhood?*
>
> *If you believe in past lives, ask: Did I come in with this from a past life?*
>
> *If the answer is yes, ask to know more about the life.*
>
> *Do I have other family members who have this tendency?*
>
> *What is the best way for me to stop myself from getting into this negative aspect?*
>
> *Is there anything else I need to know about this?*
>
> *Prioritize your list, and work with the negative tendencies that are the strongest in you by using an evening*

*review of your day and the suggestions your Higher Self
gave you.*

Now let's look at all the positive characteristics of the higher nature. Some of these are:

- The ability to love others unconditionally.
- Feeling compassion for others.
- Having a warm heart.
- Being kind and generous.
- Wanting others to succeed.
- Being helpful when someone needs help.
- Looking at things with hopefulness.
- Being calm and having serenity.
- Seeing life in a positive manner.
- Striving to be one with your spirit.

Exercise:

Make a list of what you feel are the aspects of your higher nature. Also, do a nightly review and ask yourself if during the day you displayed or felt any of these. If other positive things come up for you, add those to your list. Notice if certain people put you into one of the positive characteristics.

Then link with your Higher Self and ask it the following questions:

How strong is this tendency in me? Give it a number from one to ten, ten being the highest.

Did I develop it in my childhood?

Do I have family members who have this tendency?

If you believe in past lives, ask: Did I develop this in another life?

If the answer is yes, ask: Can I know more about the life?

Do I try to remember to be in one of these positive aspects?

If the answer is no, ask: How can I remember to do this more?
Next, prioritize your list; then take the aspects with the lowest numbers and ask your Higher Self the following questions:
How can I develop this positive aspect more?
Is anything specifically stopping me from doing this, other than my lower nature?

When you work to develop these positive aspects more fully, notice if some lower nature thoughts come up to try and stop you.

Even if you have no desire to be on a spiritual quest and simply want to open your heart more, you will still face the challenges that I have written about in this chapter. A spiritual journey isn't necessarily studying a specific religion or pursuing a specific spiritual practice. A spiritual quest could simply be the need to change some of your characteristics and become a better person; or it can be a concern about the planet or the people in third world nations who are suffering. Any altruistic practice is also a spiritual one.

The following is a story that illustrates this:

In Canada there lived a very wealthy man. James was a philanthropist who gave money to many charities around the world. One summer, he decided that it would be interesting to visit some of the countries where his money was helping. He planned to go incognito so that he could see what was really happening and not be given the grand tour by the higher-ups. He also decided to go alone, mainly because he had young children and his wife wanted to stay with them at home and not expose them to the poverty and lifestyles he was going to visit.

Most of the countries he visited were in eastern and southern Africa. He was given a couple of names of people from the charities he supported, but he decided not to look them up.

His plan was to travel by local transportation and experience what it was like to be in the area first-hand. James followed this itinerary as soon as he arrived and

found it all disgusting. He was exposed to jammed and
dirty buses and, in general, very unsanitary conditions.

James was a very fun-loving man, warm and
friendly, but as soon as he entered the first small village and started interacting with the natives, he felt
revolted. He suddenly lost his warm heart. He had no
compassion and wanted to leave as quickly as possible.
Nothing moved him. It all made him depressed, and
mainly brought up the desire to fly to a big city and
bathe in a luxurious suite at the best hotel available.
He followed this desire and flew to Johannesburg. In a
couple of days he felt more normal and could then be
warmhearted again.

He started to feel a little guilty about his attitude
toward the native people in the villages and decided to
contact the people whose names were given to him by
his charities. They were awaiting his call and immediately invited him out to dinner. The first contact was
a man named Nemo, a very distinguished black man
who ran a very large company outside of Johannesburg. He invited James on a tour of the factory and an
outing to a famous waterfall nearby.

In the next few days, James was wined and dined
and taken to scenic places. He even went on a safari
with a small group of leaders who lived there. The safari was conducted lavishly, with all the proper equipment and airtight tents. James enjoyed that the most,
and was sorry that his wife and children had not come
with him.

When it was time to return home, James said
goodbye to his new friends, He then extended the date
on his airline ticket and returned back to his original
plan. This time he hoped he would be able to see the
poverty and the unhealthy conditions without feeling
the same disgust that he had experienced before. Of
course, the conditions hadn't changed, and he found
himself again immersed in abject poverty. Where was
his money going? His hosts had told him some of the
ways it was helping, but when he went to the areas

they mentioned, there was no sign of the water stations or washing facilities they had said were brought in with his money.

He spoke to the head tribesmen of some of the most remote villages. They told him through an interpreter he had hired that they had been promised new equipment, but it was delayed to the point that they really didn't believe it would ever come. In the meantime, the unsanitary conditions were causing outbreaks of malaria, and, of course, the AIDS virus was very prevalent, with no drugs or education to change it.

During this time, even though James felt sick with the conditions, he continued his journey of exploring the areas that were supposed to be receiving the benefits of his money. The more he saw, the more irate he became not only at the charities but also at his own stupidity and reluctance to investigate the truth.

When he returned to Johannesburg, he again contacted his previous hosts and surprised them with what he had done. They explained that he must have gone to the wrong villages and that they could take him to the ones that were being helped. He knew this was a lie, and this infuriated him even more. They all lived in luxurious housing, which he realized was all probably paid for with his and others' funding.

When he returned home, he wrote a scathing article about what had happened and gave it to one of the major newspapers to publish. This, of course, caused uproar in the charities and led to an investigation of what he had seen.

Those in charge in Canada claimed they had no idea that all of this was happening. The people they had sent there in the past were shown a couple of villages that had been cleaned up and were operating with clean conditions and new schools. They had believed the representatives in Africa, who claimed that this was happening throughout many villages, not just a select few. In due time, the charities changed their personnel and brought in different people to run

the operation in Africa. In the end, James' observations
made many positive changes happen.

On his first trip to the villages, James focused on his personal discomfort and was no longer in his heart. On his second journey into the villages, James stayed in his heart. Even though the conditions were just as bad, being in his heart made him more aware of his purpose. He could then stay focused on what he had been told was happening, and what he actually saw. It was difficult for him to do, but his focused heart had only one mission, which was to change what was happening. It took courage not to run back to comfortable surroundings. This courage paid off in accomplishing his real mission of helping the natives live a more decent, disease-free life.

This story also illustrates how negative feelings can pull a person out of his heart. If James really operated with an open, warm heart all the time, then no matter what happened he would still be in his heart. Even in hardship, he would see things through the heart and want to help change such conditions. It was a good lesson for him.

When you begin to work with your heart consciously, you will feel some opposite feelings of negativity. This is a pull from your lower nature to stop you from developing your heart. When this happens, simply say no to it. Realize the importance of continuing the work. It will not only keep you focused on the positive, but it will change who you are.

Part Four: Applying Heart Energy

16

Using the Heart to Develop Your Creativity

When you use your heart on a regular basis, you start to understand how your heart functions in terms of developing your creativity. It is only through your heart that you can reach up into the higher realms and bring back ideas and inspiration that can lead to manifestations of beauty. Artists, writers, musicians, and any people who strive to bring in new ideas that can stimulate others, whether consciously or unconsciously, work with the heart to do so. Those working in the fields of science and scientific invention receive their creative ideas this way as well. Even people in the corporate world, when they use their heart in their work, produce more inventive results than when they are just using their minds.

It usually is a combination of both mind and heart that helps to take those creative ideas and manifest them in the world. A good example of someone who developed this creative inspiration is Einstein. He would lie down with metal balls in his hand. When he fell asleep, his hand would open and the balls would fall out and hit the floor, making enough noise to slightly awaken him. It was while he was in this in-between state that he would receive all the ideas that led to his theories. When he was fully awake he would write the ideas down and then use his mind to develop them.

Everyone can access these higher realms, where there is great wisdom. The heart is the conduit that brings this information to you. Many people meditate and in that process are able to receive ideas about a project they are working on. Often this information is given to a person in a way that is very individual: for example, artists may see a finished painting before they have started it and musicians can hear the music before they compose the score. Beethoven was deaf later in his life, but he would hear the whole symphony in his head and write it down, and he never did hear it when an orchestra played it.

To develop this ability takes concentration and the ability to focus with the heart on the thought that you want to develop. For example, you might need to design a plan for a product that your company is making. This could be a marketing plan or even a strategic plan outlining when and where the product will be presented. If you only use your mind to do this you can still complete the task, but it will lack the kind of energy that would attract the right audience. If instead you also worked with your heart, you would come up with unique ideas to present the product in an interesting and attractive manner.

Great visionaries work with both the mind and heart, even when they aren't aware they are doing so. It's a natural process for them, whereas most people only use their minds to develop something new.

Exercise:

> *Close your eyes and relax your body, breathing deeply, until you feel you are in a quiet, calm place. Next, link with your heart center and ask yourself the following questions:*
> *How can I develop my creativity more?*
> *Am I using my full potential when I develop an idea?*
> *If the answer is no, ask: How can I begin doing this?*
> *If the answer is yes, ask: How can I stay centered so I can make this process even*
> *stronger?*
> *When I feel inspired, do I take that inspiration and fully develop it?*
> *If the answer is no, ask: What stops me from doing this?*
> *If the answer is yes, ask: Do I always do this?*
> *If the answer is no, ask: Why not?*
> *When I have completed working on a creative idea and manifest it, do I continue to check what I have done and remain open to new ideas coming in that would im-prove my original concept?*

If the answer is no, ask: What stops me from doing this?
If the answer is yes, ask: Does this usually improve the
original idea?

Generally you will find the answer to the last question will be yes; by rechecking something, you will come up with new ideas that will not only improve your project but also develop it more strongly.

The following story illustrates this:

> Edward was a mechanical engineer for a machine manufacturing company. He designed parts that went into various types of machines, mainly large manufacturing machines.
>
> Basically, when he worked, he would develop all aspects of what the machine's function would be, starting with the smallest, simple part and moving to the most complex one. He often worked with two and sometimes three other engineers, depending on the size and complexity of the machine.
>
> For example, he and three other engineers were developing a machine that would produce wood veneer to be used on floors, tables, etc. After first being cut in big slices, the original wood had to be soaked in hot water, and then sliced thinly into large pieces and pasted onto panels that had adhesive on both sides. The last stage of the process was to cut the panels into various sizes. Each of these operations had a separate machine and required people to individually feed the slices into the appropriate machine one at a time.
>
> The team was trying to figure out a way to integrate some of the process so you wouldn't need different people to handle each part. The team consisted of Edward, the leader, David, John, and one woman, Diane, who had just joined the company. They first talked about what was needed and then did a brainstorming session in which they threw out ideas and wrote them down on a blackboard. Looking at the ideas, they then discussed the pros and cons of each, trying to determine how to make them fit into a more integrated plan.

At this point, Diane asked the group to try another process, which she called heartstorming. Edward looked at the other men with a grin on his face; "Don't you think that's a little feminine for us?"

Diane replied, "Well, I just learned it from a man who was teaching a more powerful way to do team building, which involves adding this step after the brain-storming. Do you think it's going to make you a sissy?"

David said, "There's no harm in trying it." And John nodded his head.

Edward looked disgusted, but agreed. "Okay, you're in charge, Diane."

She explained that heartstorming meant taking each of the main ideas and putting that idea into your heart and letting it go, and then being open to additional ideas coming in.

David came up with a way of connecting the soaking operation to the cutting operation. They all agreed and then took that idea, thought about it and put those results back in their hearts, and so on. The end result was far better than what they'd gotten in the original brainstorming session. Even Edward had to agree that it was a good process, and one that gave everyone a lot of energy. They ended up connecting two more processes, coming up with new machines that were much more efficient and also safer.

Of course, heartstorming as illustrated is for a group to do, but using your heart to deepen the creative process can be done individually and in any type of situation.

Exercise:

Choose something you do at work. Write it down. It can be anything from typing letters, to managing a program or a group of people.
Think about how you proceed in doing this work. What are the steps?
Write them down.
Is any part of this work creative? Write that down.

*If you feel that no part of the work is creative, look at
the work again and ask yourself why it can't be more
creative. Really explore the answer.*
*When you feel you have analyzed your work process as
much as you can, put all the results in your heart and
ask: Is there more I can do?*
*If you get an answer, think about it and then put those
thoughts back in your heart to deepen them.*

The end result should differ completely from your original process.

If your work is of a creative nature, it's important to work with your
heart to bring in more inspiration. Artists can normally do this without
thinking about what they are doing. It's part of the creative process to feel
inspired to do something and then to manifest it. The inspiration and creative ideas come from your heart and then you need to use the mind to
manifest the ideas into a product. Usually, even during this stage of man-
ifesting—for example, when the artist looks at her work or a composer
hears her work—the artist moves into the heart at times, even coming up
with new ideas as to how to improve the project. The whole process is a
back-and-forth between mind and heart.

Exercise:

*The following is a process you can do with any creative
endeavor:*
*Think about what you want to create. It can be any-
thing from painting a painting to building a bookcase;
just make it something you need to design.*
*Take the idea and put it into your heart. Also, try to
start visualizing it and how it will end up looking.*
*Take that result and write it down, or even draw it out,
working on it with the mind.*
*Take that result and put it back into your heart. If
something new comes up, write or draw that and try to
visualize the result.*

Let's say, for example, you want to paint a painting. The first stage in
your process may reveal what the subject matter will be; next, perhaps how
big it will be; and then you will start to visualize the colors you will use, etc.
If your project is a piece of music, you may start to play some of the main
themes, then write them down and later develop the ideas further.

If the project is building a bookcase, you would use the above process to decide on the wood, color, size, etc., until you come up with a final drawing of how your bookcase will look. The main thing is to go back and forth using the mind and heart to achieve the best results.

The more you work with your heart, the more you will be developing your creativity. Everything you do can have a creative element to it, whether it is cleaning your house, checking your mail or doing any other mundane thing. Looking at each task with your heart can help you tackle that task in the best way imaginable.

The creative heart can come up with new ways to solve a problem as well as give you the inspiration to move through something in a very efficient manner. The following story gives an example of what I mean:

> Around 60 years ago, Evelyn took a job in a big corporation, which required that she be in charge of the employee library. Besides ordering new books, reading and writing reviews and keeping the library orderly, she had to remind people when their books were due. Her new boss told her that none of the previous people could handle this task along with the other duties that were part of the job. He told her that he wasn't expecting her to be any different, but just to do the best she could when she had the time to work on it.
>
> Everything was in chaos. It took her several weeks just to get the library in good order and shelved correctly. Her main problem was devising a system that would tell her when the books were due. This was long before computer technology had programs that made this kind of work easy. In fact, she only had a typewriter.
>
> When she thought about it, she had some ideas, but none of them looked like they would work. Frustrated, she meditated at home and linked with her heart, asking to be inspired. She saw colored cards. The colors represented the four weeks in a month. All the books were due after one month, but if she put a person's name on a colored card for a month from now, that wouldn't relate which day the books were due.

Putting this problem into her heart again, she realized she needed color markers that indicated more accurately when a book was due. She made colored tags and numbered them one to thirty-one for the days in the month. When a new card was made, she tagged the card on top in a position according to the date. For instance, if the date were a 5, the tag would be on the left, and if it were 25, it would be on the far right. When a person took a book out, Evelyn would type up an index card for the person, put the tag on, and stamp the date on the card and also on a card in the book itself. Then she put the index card in a card file in the 4-week section. When that week was over, she would take those cards and move them to the three-week section, and so on. The week a book was due involved the one-week section, and she would call the person two days before a book was due. It was quick and easy for her to look through that section and pull a card for that date. Since there was a fine for overdue books, this procedure kept people informed. If someone didn't return a book, she stuck a colored card behind the index card so she could remind the person again. When someone renewed a book, she would enter the new date and start over again.

She had a separate file with the names of all the books in the library listed according to the section in the library; also, the date and name of the person who took each book out was listed in this file. She would tag the book if it wasn't returned and was still out. If someone else wanted a book that was out, she would place a colored card with the person's name and extension behind the relevant card.

She thought about getting a company list of names and typing up the cards ahead of time, but she realized that not everyone took out books. When a book was returned, she filed the name alphabetically to be used the next time the person took a book out.

Evelyn was studying art at night and often had to stay up late doing homework, so once the system was

in place, many times she would take a book and pretend she was reading it to review and take a short nap.
Some workers caught her doing this and reported it
to her boss. He said, "Are you kidding? She is the only
person that could ever do this job! If she sleeps once in
a while, that's fine with me."

Because Evelyn was a creative person, she easily used her creativity to
make an impossible job possible.

Exercise:

*Think of anything in your life that you feel needs to be
changed but you don't really know how to make changes.*
*Think about it and write down all the details that need
to be changed.*
*Then put it all in your heart and ask: What's the best
way for me to go about making these changes?*
*Do the heart/mind system until you come up with what
feels like the best solution.*

When you bring creativity into any process, it opens you to all possibilities. Anything that seems too difficult or impossible can really have a
creative solution to make it possible. Never put a final evaluation on a difficult situation and close the door to changing it. Keeping that door open
helps you to tap the creative source through your heart. The heart brings in
the inspiration and the creative plan and the mind puts it into action. This
is a balance of the feminine and masculine within everyone. Much is lost
when you use only the mind to resolve.

17

Using the Heart in Your Work

Trying to remember to be in your heart while you are working is often very difficult. Anything that is work-related, unless it is creative work, is usually mental. It is also difficult because work-related conversations with co-workers, as well as meetings with strangers, are often part of the day. Depending on your job, you might be in your mind 95% of the time.

This happens with any service type of job.

If you are in sales, which is people-oriented, you can try to be more in your heart, but the selling part often puts you into the mind rather than the heart.

If you are attending college or university, the work is intellectual. Exams and reports are analytical and require concentrated mental work.

How to change the mind orientation is a key question, especially if you are in one of the above situations. Here are several things you can do consciously.

1. When you are having a business-related conversation, before speaking, link with your heart and try to link with the heart of the person you are speaking to.

2. When you are writing a report or doing anything analytical, take the time to first link with your heart and ask that you remember to take any information that you are thinking about and place it in your heart to deepen it.

3. When you are talking to several people at a meeting, just before your meeting link with your heart and then with your Higher Self, and ask that you are clear in your responses and that you use your heart in the process.

4. When you are with someone who is very intellectual, connect with your heart as you listen so that your response can be enhanced.

5. When you need to listen to someone who has complaints, try to be in your heart and experience his feelings and real needs, so you can respond accordingly.

6. If you are studying for a test, ask your Higher Self to help you in the work, and focus on your heart when you answer the test questions.

7. If you have to be in a debate, try to remember to be in your heart and listen to the other debaters with your heart.

8. If you have a sales job and are presenting goods to someone, link with your heart and ask if this product is good for the person. If not, ask what product would be better.

9. Start each day with a quiet moment of linking with your heart and telling yourself to remember to be in your heart throughout the day.

10. Lastly, in the evening, do the nightly review, looking back on the day to determine how often you remembered to be in your heart.

So much of this work takes practice, especially for those people who don't naturally work with their hearts.

Exercise:

> *Do the process to link with your heart.*
> *Take each item on the above list that relates to you*
> *and ask: Is there anything stopping me from doing this*
> *technique?*
> *If you get a yes, then ask: What is the block and how do*
> *I overcome it?*

When there is a lot of resistance, it may be necessary to ask the Higher Self for details on how the resistance came about. Knowing the basic cause of a problem can really be helpful in overcoming it. The following story is an example of inner resistance:

> On the Gulf of Mexico there lived a young woman named Adelita. She was a very beautiful woman with striking black hair and eyes and a fiery, passionate temperament. For her to be in her heart was difficult because her emotions were always out there, keeping her overly expressive. At the time of this story, her mother had just died and Adelita, at the age of eighteen, was confronted with having to take care of her two younger siblings, both girls. Her father worked long hours and could be of no help in raising his daughters.
>
> Adelita felt stuck and resented having to take over her mother's job. She basically wanted to work, have fun and date young men who wanted adventure. Her mother, on her deathbed, made Adelita swear to fulfill her last wish, which was to be in charge of the household.
>
> During the day Adelita worked, then she came home and took care of her sisters, made dinner, cleaned up, and did most of the housework. When her father came home late at night, she took off to a party or to be with friends. Naturally, she got little sleep and was exhausted each morning when she went to her job as a secretary.
>
> One day her boss called her in and told her that if she did not improve her attitude and her work, she would be fired. The family had very little money, so she knew they could not afford to lose the money she brought home, most of which she turned over to her father. She realized that to keep her job, she had to get more sleep and not be so resentful all the time. She previously had a good relationship with her boss, but now it had deteriorated, with her snapping at him.
>
> But how could she change? If she gave up her partying then she wouldn't have a life, yet it would be impossible to become even poorer than the family already was. Her sisters were trying to help more,

but they were only ten and twelve and had homework every night.

What to do? In her dilemma, she decided to talk to a co-worker, a young married woman who had just joined the company. Juanita was a nice woman, kind and openhearted. They talked and Juanita said, "What does your heart tell you to do to keep your job and do all the work that is required of you?"

"My heart, what do you mean, my heart? What does my heart have to do with this?"

"The heart can be a great help. Any problem can be solved by the heart."

"Really? That's hard to believe. How can my heart help me?"

"First you must try to become calm. You are always so emotional, and the emotions will stop you from listening to your heart."

"Calm, that's impossible for me. I'm made this way."

"You may be born with certain tendencies, but you don't have to hold on to the ones that aren't helping you."

Juanita then gave Adelita a basic exercise on how to calm down her emotions. She told her to sit quietly, link with her heart and feel that all her emotions were becoming part of a big black ball forming in her heart. She was to then imagine taking that black ball and throwing it into the sun above.

Then Juanita told her, "Once you feel calm, then link with your heart and ask yourself, 'How can I change my attitude at my work so I can keep this job?'"

Adelita did this and thought, "I need to let go of my resentment toward my father and my mother for making me do this."

Then, with Juanita coaching her, she asked herself, "How can I do this?"

The answer surprised her: "Remember, you have a heart, but you need to learn how to use it correctly."

With Juanita's help, she came up with a first step. Instead of responding to every situation in a loud, demonstrative manner, she needed to link with her heart and respond softly, with focus.

She practiced first with her sisters. She usually yelled at them, but she decided to stop, as it was not their fault that she had to take care of them. Her resentment toward them was hurtful to them also. Previously, their relationship was a good one, but now it was all harsh words. When she stopped yelling, they no longer yelled either, and soon the situation was better. They even offered to help her more now that they were not being bossed into doing things.

Her father was a different story. She basically never talked to him anymore. She just treated him coldly, with no love or affection. He was a nice man, but he was also burdened with his loss and his long working hours. When she started to treat him more kindly and talked to him, he stopped coming home so late; much of his time after work had been spent drinking with his friends. He also started to help her more by shopping and cleaning up. Dinner again became a family affair, something that hadn't happened since the mother died.

Every time she became emotional, she would do the exercise, take some deep breaths, and tell herself to stay in her heart.

What she did at home soon reflected in her behavior at her job, and her boss noticed the difference and complimented her on it.

Later, when her sisters grew older, they did more and more of the work, freeing her to go out normally and have more fun. When her father met and married another woman, Adelita moved out and lived with a friend, eventually getting married herself.

Working on using her heart not only changed Adelita's personality, but it also helped her to reach out to others more and to love her family.

When you work with your heart at the office, remember that not everyone is going to respond to heart energy. For instance, someone who is very mental needs to relate through the mind and has a difficult time responding to heart energy. When you have someone like this in your life, especially at work, try to recognize the best method to relate to that person. You want to eventually use your heart energy with such a person, but you may have to work up to this slowly. If, for example, you have a co-worker like this and you are consciously sending heart energy to that person, he may feel there is something wrong with you, that you have become too sweet. It could create suspicion about whether or not you can do your job. Be nice, be in your heart, but speak to the person with a combination of heart and mind.

Often, having to evaluate the right approach can be confusing. I suggest doing the following exercise:

Exercise:

> Think of the words you generally use when you are speaking to someone, and write them down. Study your list.
>
> Do you use more heart-oriented words, or are they more mind-oriented? Rate yourself from one to ten on each word that is more heart-oriented, ten representing the highest degree of heart energy. Then do the same for the words that are more mind-oriented. Check your ratings with your Higher Self.
>
> Then make a list of all the people you have to work with or deal with in your job. Next to each name, write an evaluation of the person's energy. Is this person more heart-oriented? Mark a number from one to ten, ten being the highest rating. Then ask if the person is more mind-oriented. Rate that person, again from one to ten, regarding where his energy lies.

When talking to someone who is more heart-oriented, use heart words, such as feel, desire, or experience––anything that is expressive. If the person is more mind-oriented, use words like think, believe, or know––anything that is analytical. Try listening to each type of person. You will discover that the person will automatically use words that describe where his energy is. If you only use words related to who you are and those words are the opposite of the other person's inclinations, he will not have an easy time responding to you.

Exercise:

>*Look at your list of people from the previous exercise, and choose one person who has a high rating in either the mind or heart. When you next speak to this person, try to notice the kinds of words he uses. After the conversation, mark those words next to his name, and then try to remember to use those kinds of words the next time you meet.*

It's best to try this with one person at a time until you are used to listening in this manner and have practiced the right responses. The next person you choose to work with should be the opposite. If you started out with a heart person, choose someone who is more mind-oriented next.

This can become a fun game to play, and you may be surprised to discover that someone you thought was warm hearted speaks more from the mind, and vice versa.

If someone rates in the middle in both energies, e.g., a 4, 5, or 6, then try to talk to that person using an equal amount of both types of words. This is a greater challenge, as you have to combine the techniques. If you yourself are someone with a mix, then it will be easier for you to do.

To change your way of speaking takes a great deal of self-awareness. After you have had a conversation with someone, check if you used words that were geared toward that person. Notice when you have slipped into your own style of speaking.

Start this practice with the people you work with. You generally have more contact with them and can practice daily. Once you feel comfortable with moving back and forth between the two modalities, you can then continue this work with a list of friends and family.

Remember, even while you are talking to someone in the mind-oriented modality, it's important for you to be in your heart and put the warmth of your heart in the words that you express. You can do this in the following manner:

- Link with your heart before entering the conversation.

- When appropriate, ask your Higher Self to send heart vibrations to the person you are talking to.

- If for some reason you talk in a way that brings you out of your heart, try to link again with your heart.

Sometimes, in an animated conversation, you may start to be all in the mind. It's therefore important to slow down and remember that speaking quickly can take you out of your heart and into the mind.

Another thing that can take you out of your heart is feeling tired, irritated, or emotional; eventually what happens is there is a shift from the positive heart energy to negative feelings or feelings that are exaggerated. When this happens, it is difficult to remember to disidentify and become calm. Try to pause, take some deep breaths, and link with your Higher Self. Then, when you feel calmer, link with your heart. Negative emotions coming into your heart will flood it and block its pure energy.

Exercise:

> *Link with your heart and ask yourself the following questions:*
> *Is there anyone I work with who causes me to become emotional?*
> *If the answer is yes, write down the name or names.*
> *Take a name on your list and ask:*
> *Why does this person bring up my emotions?*
> *Is there any way I can stop this from happening?*
> *If I am in these emotions, what is the best way for me to release them?*
> *How can I prepare myself before meeting with this person?*
> *Do this exercise with each name on the list, one at a time, and remember to do the preparation step before meeting with the person. Practicing this even for a short time helps you to stay in your heart.*

When you work with people on a daily basis, many challenges emerge, especially if your work involves dealing with many people. These challenges can best be approached if you stay in your heart. The heart always knows the right way to solve a problem or the correct way to accomplish a task. Keep working with your heart, not just with loved ones, but also with those you have to deal with in your job.

18

Using the Heart to Understand Your Environment

When you are striving to live from your heart, it is important to look at what surrounds you as well as your inner life and your relationships with people. Living in a place that is clean, tidy, and beautiful makes it much easier to be in your heart. Obviously, beauty is different for each person. What you consider beautiful may not be liked at all by someone else. Realize that beauty is a quality, and when it surrounds you, it makes you feel happier and more loving. And mainly, beauty uplifts your spirit.

Sometimes it takes time to get to know what your likes and dislikes are. Also, as you grow older, what you felt was beautiful when you were young may no longer seem so. If this is the case for you, it is important to rid yourself of those objects that you no longer care for.

Re-evaluating how you are living and what you have in the way of possessions on a yearly basis is a very useful practice. Objects in a home can also be rearranged and take on a new appearance in a different room or setting.

Naturally, this refers to your own likes and dislikes. If you have a partner, obviously what she feels is beautiful may differ from your view. Let's look at the areas that you need to examine in terms of beauty in your home environment:

- The type of art you have around you.

- The colors of the rooms and furniture.
- The style of furnishings.
- The design and layout of the rooms.
- The way the rooms are decorated.
- The ways that you bring in nature, such as with flowers or plants.
- The type of energy that is there.

When someone looks at her environment, she often sees it in practical terms. How easy is it to find something? What is the condition of the furnishings? What needs to happen for the environment to function better? Even little things are connected to the ebb and flow of the energy.

All of the above needs to feel positive in order to bring a sense of beauty into your home.

Exercise:

> *Look at the list above and see how you feel about each item, rating each from one to ten, ten being the highest positive rating. Then prioritize your list, putting the lowest-rated items on top. Next, take each one that is rated seven or lower; link with your heart and ask: Why don't I like this aspect of my home? What bothers me?*
> *If you live with someone, ask: Is this my partner's taste? Is there any way I can change this?*
> *If it is all right with your partner, ask: What is the best way for me to go about doing this?*
> *Does the energy in the room feel good to me?*
> *If it does not, ask: How can I best change that?*
> *If it is not possible to change it, ask: How can I accept it as it is?*
> *If you can never accept it, ask: What would be a first step in creating a better environment of my own?*

If you live with someone who has completely different tastes, then it is best to work together and negotiate in order to have some of the preferences of each person represented in the design and atmosphere of your space. In many cases, you and your partner will have separate offices or work areas. In that arrangement, you can completely decorate your own space the way you like. If the mix in the other rooms starts to bother you, then just going into your own space will make you feel better.

It's also important to stay in your heart when you look at something that you don't like, and just accept that your partner really loves it and therefore you can accept it. If you find that your partner doesn't like something of yours, try to talk with her about it. If the issue can't be resolved, just let the object go or put it in your own office space. If it is big, such as a piece of furniture, try to replace it with something you both can agree upon. Often major fights in a partnership come from small things, so try always to step back from a situation and not battle it out when it's not really that important.

Naturally, if your partner has to have everything her way, you may need to have an outside person mediate the situation. Look at the material objects in your surroundings simply as objects that can be there or not, according to various tastes. Remember, nothing is as important as maintaining a calm and loving atmosphere in the home you live in.

If for some reason you do have an argument with your partner, or even a roommate, try to settle it amiably right away, and then, at another time, burn sage or incense in the room where you had the argument. Doing this removes any negative vibrations that were left there. Tell your partner why you are doing this, or she may become offended.

Your environment doesn't always just include the adults you live with. If you have children living in your home, it's important that they also learn to keep the house neat and orderly. Any mess is negative and brings in negative vibrations that affect everyone living there. Teach your children to have neat habits, and always praise them for this. Even children who are messy feel better when they clean up their rooms. Teach them the importance of throwing out things they are not using. A good example of this is the following story:

> Mildred was a mother of seven children. They all shared rooms, except for the eldest, who had a small room of his own. Mildred really tried her best to teach all her children good manners and to have a clean environment in the home. Unfortunately, her oldest child always rebelled against tidying his room and never listened to her or her husband concerning cleanliness. Both parents were upset at the mess that was always in

his room. His siblings all tried to follow their parents' direction, but Sam, the oldest, never did.

When Sam was eighteen, he went away to college and lived in a dorm with another student, equally as untidy. Their room reeked with negative vibrations, and after a while, none of their friends wanted to visit them. When they went to their friends' rooms, they would leave a mess of coke cans and paper wrappings behind, which started to irritate others.

Soon they were being avoided and dropped from the regular crowd. Sam finally asked a friend, who still stayed in contact with him, what had happened, for he had thought that he was well liked and socially accepted. When his friend told him it was because his room was so dirty and messy and because he also left other rooms that way, Sam was aghast. At first he rebelled, which was his usual reaction, but then he started to look around him and realized how much his room smelled with old food wrappers. He cleaned up everything in his area, but his roommate's part of the room remained dirty. Later, he told his roommate that they had to change the way they lived. He also, by the way, had a difficult time studying in his room and generally did that at the school library.

His roommate argued with him and said that it was none of Sam's business how he kept his part of the room, and that, in fact, he had learned his messiness from Sam. A big quarrel ensued, and Sam went to the school authorities and asked to be given another roommate. When the person in charge checked with the students who still needed roommates, she was surprised when they all said no. Sam was nice, but he was too much a slob for any of them to live with. Sam was told this and agreed that it was true, but he said that he wanted to change and become neater; would someone give him a chance? There was a new student who had just arrived mid-term who agreed to try the living arrangement with Sam. It worked out very well, as Sam was determined to keep his portion of the room neat

and the new student was a good example of this. When
the new roommate invited some friends to their room,
some who knew Sam were surprised at how neat his
section was and even congratulated him. Soon, Sam
was again active with his friends, but his old roommate
was still not included in most of the activities.

This is just a small example, and one that ended well, but in reality,
most people who spend their childhood living in messy conditions carry
this habit with them throughout their lives. Sam had an easier time changing this because the rest of his family had always been neat. At times, when
someone is raised in a messy environment, she will do the opposite as an
adult, making her surroundings super neat and orderly; but usually, the
messy habit prevails and carries on.

Exercise:

> *If you are messy rather than neat, ask yourself the fol-*
> *lowing questions:*
> *Was my environment growing up mainly neat and or-*
> *derly, or was it the opposite, messy and disorderly?*
> *If the answer is the latter, ask: Can I change this and*
> *not follow the habit of being disorderly?*
> *If you feel you can change this and want to do that, ask*
> *yourself: What is the best plan for me to begin to change*
> *this habit?*
> *Write the plan down carefully, and then ask your*
> *Higher Self: Is this plan the best one for me to follow?*
> *If the answer is no, ask: What would be a better plan?*
> *If you receive a better plan, reflect on it, and ask your*
> *Higher Self any questions that you need to in order to*
> *clarify it better.*

Often someone makes a plan that looks good on paper, but in reality,
it is initially too difficult to follow, particularly if you have a negative habit
that first needs to change in order to accomplish your goal. An example
would be someone who wants to clean out her closets and drawers but
has a difficult time throwing things out. This person may have good intentions, but she is too attached to keeping stuff that she never even looks at.
Everyone has someone in the family who is like this. Clutter is the hardest

thing to eliminate. This habit concerns attachments, attachments that hold a person bound in turmoil and disorder.

The following is a useful exercise.

Exercise:

> *Find a quiet, calm place. Sit and link with your heart and your Higher Self. Close your eyes and imagine you are in your home office or bedroom. Walk around the room, noticing the things that are there. How often do you look at them? Do they bring beauty to your room? For each thing that doesn't, ask yourself:*
>
> *Why do I keep this? Does it have sentimental value for me?*
>
> *If that answer is a yes, ask yourself: Do I really need this, or is there something else that I own that gives me the same sentimental feeling that would be more important to keep?*
>
> *Really be honest with yourself when you ask: Can I literally do without this?*
>
> *If you feel you can do without it, then either sell it or give it to someone else who would value it.*

People's attics and basements are full of such stuff. Unless everything is kept neatly on shelves, negative vibrations are attracted, and those vibrations can adversely affect the people who are near them.

Unfortunately, if someone becomes a pack rat, that person believes that everything she owns is important and will be concerned if her partner throws something out. Fights occur around this, and marriages can break up when one partner is neat and the other is messy.

The reason why a neat, clean environment is important when working with the heart is that negative vibrations in your surroundings will interfere with you being connected to your heart. Even when your surroundings are beautiful and orderly, if someone fights or is irritated in that space, your environment will be negatively affected; those negative vibrations need to be cleared out. Usually, the best way to do that is to use sage, which is a purifier. Also, having roses in the room helps to change any negativity.

It is especially important to keep your work area beautiful and neat. If you have flowers in it, be certain to clean the water on a regular basis. Doing this helps the flowers and keeps the water from becoming stagnant and smelly. Some people burn incense when they work. Incense is also a good purifier.

If you meditate, make certain that the area you use is positive in feeling. Flowers, incense and candles help to make that happen.

Also, if you have young children, sometimes they fight and squabble. Telling them to stop doesn't necessarily work. Just burn sage to clear the air; then, when they are older, talk with them about keeping their environment clean. They may not care about it, but you can ask them to honor your wishes. Mainly, if you set a good example, your children will notice and usually follow it.

The other aspect of the home environment that sometimes needs to be purified occurs when you have certain animals. Generally animals are fine, especially if they are loved and taken good care of, but if you have too many of them, they can often get negative. For example, some cats really don't like each other or don't like being near a dog. Having one or two that get along or just ignore each other is fine, but some people will take in four or more cats. This causes dissension and can even cause a dirty environment, especially if their litter box is not cleaned out daily. If you have gone into someone's house that is like that, you will understand what I mean. Many dogs, rabbits, or even birds can cause the same type of chaos, which not only negatively affects the humans living there but also any other animals.

This chapter is about living in beauty. It's about building an atmosphere around you that makes you feel happy, calm, safe, and comfortable. It's about working on producing positive effects for all the people living in and entering your home. Having fun, laughing, feeling happy—all of these bring qualities that make your place wonderful to be in.

Exercise:

> *Ask yourself the following questions:*
> *When I am in my home, do I generally feel content and happy?*
> *Do I often laugh and enjoy myself there with friends and family?*
> *Do I look forward to spending time there, even if I live alone?*
> *When I am home, is there anything there that annoys me?*
> *When I am home, are there things there that bring me pleasure?*

Do I feel that my home is truly a place I want to be?
Do I feel comfortable inviting friends over?
When I am at home, can I sit and look at my place with
feelings of acceptance?
Do I ever want to find another place to live that would
be better?
If you answered no to any of the first eight questions
or yes to the ninth, then link with your heart and ask
yourself why you feel this way. If the why brings out an
answer that you feel you can change, then work with
your heart to understand the best way to do this.

Basically, it's important to always live in an environment that has beauty and a quiet atmosphere. This helps you to do your work and to socialize in a happy manner.

It's difficult, with a busy lifestyle, to always be aware when things change in your environment. It would be helpful to ask yourself the question, "How does it feel here?" on a regular basis. Check with your heart; your heart knows when things are calm and focused, and when that changes. Know the importance of having a good and happy relationship with whomever you live with, and realize that if this is not possible, maybe you have to change the living conditions to help make that happen.

19

Using the Heart to Better Your Way of Living

You may wonder what bettering your way of living means. The following story is an example of this:

> In the Middle Ages, people lived in very difficult circumstances. There were serfdoms where peasants tilled the fields and lived in small houses that were heated by wood fireplaces. These houses were usually just one room where the whole family lived, ate, and slept, with no privacy at all. Poverty was at its worst. Some people worked from dawn to dusk tending livestock and fields for their landowners, who owned all the land and most of the produce that came from it. The landowners always had soldiers who watched to make certain that no peasants sold any of the goods or left their homesteads. The serfs, and any children born to them, were all bonded to the landowner.
>
> It seemed impossible for any of them to be free or to better their lives—but one family did.
>
> Jacques was a peasant who lived in the south of France with his wife Maria and their three children, a son and two daughters. The whole family worked in the fields. The father and son worked there all day,

and the wife and daughters worked part of the day in the fields and the rest of the day tending the livestock, mostly chickens that produced eggs for the master's house.

Jacques had learned to read when he was a child, and he was determined to teach his wife and children. Late in the evening after dinner, when all the chores were done, they all sat down at the table for their lesson. The only book Jacques had was the Bible, so they took turns reading it. When they read about Jesus and his love for all people, they were very touched by his words and teaching. They decided to try to follow his teachings and use their hearts throughout the day. Every night they would exchange stories of how they did this. For instance, if a soldier rode by, instead of being frightened of him—the usual reaction of most of the peasants—they made a point of stopping his horse and talking with the soldier. Soon, all the soldiers on patrol knew this family and liked them. On occasion, the soldiers would stop at their house and have tea. They even brought bread and cakes to share.

When special house servants picked up the eggs during the day, Maria and her daughters would smile and talk with them. The daughters were teenagers and very pretty; some of the younger guards became interested in them, even though they were peasants and part of a lower class. Because of this difference, one of the guards had to ask permission from the landowner to marry the eldest daughter. The landowner became curious and decided to visit the family himself after the guard praised her and her kind, courteous family.

He arrived in the evening when they were doing their Bible reading. Maria and Jacques greeted him kindly. Again, because they were in their hearts, they had no fear of him. He felt their warmth, which was a new experience for him, and when they explained that they were doing their daily reading, he was quite astonished. He also saw how well kept the house was.

There were cut flowers on the table and the bedding was hidden in a corner so as not to clutter the room.

He sat down with them for tea and talked with them about their work. Jacques was very articulate, and when the landowner asked him if anything had to be improved, Jacques gave his observations about the land needing more fertilizer and what he thought would help the produce grow better.

The landowner went home and thought about this strange meeting and what had occurred. Not only did he approve of the guard's marrying the daughter, but he also promoted Jacques to the position of overseer and gave him more money and a new house with several rooms. In time, the landowner enjoyed Jacques' company more and more, and even let him take books from his library for the family to read. The whole family benefited from consciously working with Jesus' teachings on using the heart to love one another.

Someone consciously using his heart when speaking with others makes a very big difference in the way people respond. When heart energy is focused on another person, this gives the receiver a sense of being listened to and also a sense of warmth. The one using heart energy is always thought of as 'that person with a warm heart,' and because of that, the person is very much welcomed by most people.

Having such a heart quality opens all kinds of possibilities. One example is that of a television commentator. You can tell if the person is genuine. If he has a good heart quality that shines through, you want to listen to what he has to say. You can also tell when someone is cold and distant. He may be giving the news in a genuine and interesting manner, but if his heart quality isn't good, what he is saying may not seem important.

So much depends on the heart quality in every profession, particularly in the medical profession. Generally people look at doctors in a different manner than they look at most people. A doctor who is warmhearted gets a much better response than one who is businesslike and distant. Particularly when a person is very ill, he needs to feel that the doctor cares about him. Unfortunately, many doctors don't have what is called a good bedside manner, which in actuality means a positive heart quality.

Exercise:

> *Ask yourself the following questions:*
> *Have you ever had anyone say to you that you were warmhearted?*
> *Do you consciously feel warmth in your heart when you talk with someone?*
> *Do you display warmth to your close friends?*
> *Are you aware of others who have this quality?*
> *What is your general response to someone who is warmhearted?*
> *What is your general response to someone who is more distant?*
> *If you feel you do not have a warm heart, ask your Higher Self the following questions:*
> *Is there something blocking me from having a warm heart?*
> *If the answer is yes, ask: What is it?*
> *If the answer is no, ask: How can I develop this more?*

Sometimes a person has a good heart quality but hasn't tried to use it simply because he has never thought about developing it.

One reason it is so necessary to have a good heart quality is that it will help in the work you need to do. When a person goes on an interview for a job, a positive heart quality makes a difference in the interviewer's response; often someone who doesn't have as many qualifications will land a job because of this. Also, work in any kind of office can lead to promotions when someone is liked and is a good co-worker. These are important qualities that are necessary in any kind of leadership role. If you remember past Presidents of the United States, you mainly remember the ones who had this quality. Some call it charisma, but charisma basically is having a warm heart. If the above exercise made you feel that you needed to develop your heart more fully, it's important to understand not only how to do this, but also what in your past history kept you from developing it previously. Generally, if someone had parents who lacked warm hearts, the resultant basic conditioning would make it harder for the person to develop such warmth. But, if you had even one parent who was warmhearted, you would be more likely to feel the importance of that and want to emulate that parent.

Exercise:

> *Ask yourself the following question:*
> *Did I have a parent or a very close relative who was*
> *warmhearted when I was a child?*
> *If the answer is yes, ask: Who was it? And was I able to*
> *feel that warmheartedness? If so, what was that like for*
> *me?*
> *Then ask: Did I in any way want to be like that person?*
> *If the answer is no, ask: Why not?*
> *Also ask: Did I ever meet someone with that true, un-*
> *tarnished warmhearted quality when*
> *I was a child?*
> *If you did, think about the person and ask yourself if*
> *you ever wondered why that person was different from*
> *your parents and close relatives.*

Usually if someone grew up in a household with people who were not warmhearted, they were instead raised by people who mainly worked with their minds. Everything was thought-out and mental. This mind-orientation is not wrong, but it needs the heart to make it more balanced. Someone who has both the heart and mind developed can be truly creative and inspirational and also follow through to produce results. Having only one aspect, either all heart or all mind, can cause an imbalance of energies. If someone is all heart-oriented, he can have great creative ideas, but he cannot follow through and make them manifest. If someone is the opposite and only uses the mind, he will not be very creative; he can manifest things, but they lack the spark of inspiration. The following story is an example:

> Stephen was a very creative person. He was involved in painting, writing and several other arts. All his work was very inspirational and admired by his friends. His main trouble was a lack of focus when it came to promoting his work or even taking it around to galleries for shows. He made his livelihood doing carpentry, but his main work was in the arts. He was good at designing furniture and building it, but, again, he didn't have any business skills and had no idea how to try to market his work. Basically, he lacked the mental ability to follow through and create a business.

Fortunately, after many years of carpentry, he met someone who loved his designs, and that person started to market his products. The business became a success right away, and Stephen could finally stop his carpentry work and concentrate on designing and making furniture.

If he had never met such a person, he would never have been successful and wouldn't have fulfilled his destiny. Unfortunately, stories such as this happen often, and usually, there is no successful ending. That is why it's important to have both the heart and the mind developed in order to do the work you are meant to do.

Exercise:

> *Ask your Higher Self the following questions:*
> *Do I have a balance of the heart and mind that is good enough to do the work I am meant to do?*
> *If the answer is yes, ask: Is one less developed than the other?*
> *If the answer is yes, ask: Which one, and what do I need to do to develop it more?*
> *If the answer is no, there is not a good enough balance, ask: Which aspect do I need to develop more fully?*
> *Then ask for a process and a first step to begin this process.*

This book focuses on the heart. If your Higher Self responds that you need to develop the mind more, then it's important to research the different methods that are available to help you.

Using your heart to better your way of life not only refers to the vocation you pursue but also to the people in your life. If you live with someone, it is most important to be warmhearted and to listen with your heart. When you respond with a warm heart to someone, that not only creates a calming effect but it also gives the recipient a sense of belonging and a deeper sense of being cared for.

Exercise:

> *List the people you are close to and ask yourself the following questions, taking each name one at a time:*
> *Do I try to be warmhearted with this person?*

> *If the answer is no, ask: Why not?*
> *Also ask: How can I change this?*
> *Sometimes the people we care for the most are the ones*
> *we treat the worst.*
> *Again, look at each name, and determine if you treat*
> *this person badly.*
> *If so, ask: Why do I do this?*
> *Then ask: Do I want to change this?*
> *If the answer is yes, ask: What is a process to change*
> *this?*
> *If the answer is no, ask: Why don't I want to change it?*

If you find you don't want to change your treatment of someone, really examine why you feel this way toward the person. If it is someone you are close to, then having a closed-down attitude toward the person can become a problem. Maybe you then need to determine if you really want to continue to be with this person. If it is someone you have to be with, such as a close relative, maybe you need to have a talk with him to try to resolve any differences. If for some reason that can't happen, then you need to either change your attitude and be more positive, or distance yourself from the person as much as possible.

Sometimes you may find yourself in a difficult living situation that can't be changed at the present time. Simply focusing in your heart and trying to be warmhearted can help to ease the situation. Even a very negative person responds to heart energy. Also, by being in your heart, you can better understand what is happening, and that may help change the vibrations.

Heart energy can change negative vibrations. If you enter a room and are sensitive to the negative vibrations that you feel, then do the following exercise:

Exercise:

> *Connect with your heart and imagine that positive*
> *energy is flowing through it and out into the room.*
> *Use your mind to focus the energy to every corner of*
> *the room and also to move it inward to the center of*
> *the room. Imagine the energy is flowing in a circular*
> *movement throughout the room. If there are people in*
> *the room, see the energy flowing around them one at a*
> *time. Ask that your energy heal and change the negative*
> *vibrations and make the room's vibrations positive.*

The above exercise is good to do if you are in a place in which people are arguing or upset about something.

Remember that having a warm heart means you are bringing in warm energy and having it flow outwards to others as well as to your surroundings. Not only will this produce a more positive atmosphere, but it will also help you have better living conditions.

Part Five: Looking Within

Nanette V. Hucknall

20

Reconnecting to the Heart When You Are Out of Balance

Working with your heart is always a positive action, but there will be times when you may be feeling negative or moody or upset about something that is happening in your life. Obviously, if you use your heart to understand what is happening it will be most helpful, but because of your feelings, you may find yourself blocked from using your heart. It's difficult for someone to connect to her heart when she feels angry, upset or even out of sorts. She is in her lower nature and cannot connect to her heart from that place. There are exercises you can do, but before that, let's look at what happens in your body.

If you are in your lower nature, your body feels tense, upset, and rigid. You can have strong energy, but it is negative energy, so you may feel that nothing is going to be okay in your life. This type of energy keeps you down and depressed, and for some people it makes them angry and loud. These are the times when you may lash out at those you love and also feel the world is against you.

Everyone goes through such periods in their lives. It happens more with some than with others, and even the most loving and positive person can feel dark moods from time to time. Fortunately, most people go through such moods and come out of them quickly. But other people get stuck for days. These people may need medication to be lifted out of the doldrums.

Typically, when someone gets depressed and negative, she can recover in a couple of days. What needs to happen is a shift in intent. The shift can only take place if a person really wants to change her mood. Let's do an exercise to discover how you handle being in a negative place.

Exercise:

> *Ask yourself the following questions:*
> *When I feel down, how long do I generally stay that way?*
> *If I am feeling upset or angry, how long do I hold onto those feelings?*
> *Is there something in me that can help me change my mood more quickly?*
> *If the answer is yes, ask: What is it?*
> *If the answer is no, ask: Is there something I can do to change my mood?*
> *When I feel down and depressed, do I try to change to a more positive mood?*
> *If the answer is yes, ask: What do I generally do?*
> *If the answer is no, ask: Why not?*
> *Is there a common theme that happens when I am feeling negative?*
> *If the answer is yes, write down what it is and ask more about it.*
> *If the answer is no, ask: Is there a common mood I get into?*
> *How do I respond if someone tries to help me at such a time?*
> *If the response is positive, ask if it applies to a specific person.*
> *If the respond is negative, ask: Why do I not accept help?*

Many times when someone is in a bad mood, the person turns down any help offered. This usually has to do with the inability of the depressed person to allow anyone into her life. Such a person shuts herself up, doesn't go out and wants to isolate herself. This is usually not a good thing. A depressed person needs outside help but may isolate herself for days at a time even when she could return to normal just by talking with another person.

The best way to change moods is by reconnecting with your heart. The way to do this needs to be clear in your mind, and when I say clear, I mean writing down your method of connecting and putting the paper some place so you can see it easily. The bad mood will deflect you from remembering how to do this. The following steps are positive ones to take to lift you out of any negative mood.

- Listen to music that you love to hear.
- Go for a walk and try to connect with nature.
- Look at artwork you love and breathe in its beauty.
- If you know the mood concerns a certain person, then resolve to speak with her as soon as you feel more positive. If for some reason you cannot do that, then speak with a friend about the person. Mainly talk out the feelings, preferably with the person involved.
- Once you have done the above, ask your Higher Self what else you need to do to lift away the negative feelings.
- Take that answer and do it.
- Lastly, when you feel more positive, link with your heart and ask the Higher Self to let you feel the warmth of your heart.

When you feel you are back in your normal condition, stay that way for a few days and try to feel the difference. Then, when you are ready, take the time to analyze why you fell into such a mood.

Exercise:

Ask yourself the following questions:
What caused this to happen to me?
Why did I let myself fall into the mood?
How could I have handled it differently?
Did I need to have this happen to me?
Could I in any way have prevented it?
Do I have some kind of buy-in around it, something I
gain from it?
Did I try to change my mood consciously?

Did I seek help when I needed to?
Now that I am through this, can I resolve the problem
that started it in the first place?
If the problem cannot be resolved, am I able to under-
stand it enough so that it won't pull me down again?

Sometimes situations happen that can't be changed, but you can change your attitude toward them and make them more manageable. The following is a story that illustrates this:

A woman named Maryanne grew up in a small town in the west. She hated her environment, and as soon as she was old enough, she left home to go to a New York City college. She loved school and she loved living in New York. Her major was biology, and she went on to receive a Ph.D. in that field. After graduation, she found a research job in her college. Everything in her life was great. She loved her work and she was engaged to a very nice man–Andrew.

Then her life went through drastic changes. Her family at home consisted of her parents and her two younger siblings. Maryanne wasn't close to any of them, and in fact, she could no longer relate to them at all. Both her parents worked in a small factory in town, and her siblings, though still young, didn't seem interested in anything. She always went home for the holidays, and generally, she was bored there.

Disaster struck the family. Both her parents were killed in an automobile accident, and her younger sister was badly injured. Maryanne was left in charge of what remained. The little money that was there paid for the funerals, and then she was faced with what to do with her siblings. Her injured sister was fourteen at the time and would be in a wheelchair for months, or maybe longer. Her brother was sixteen and was very withdrawn. He would not speak to anyone, particularly Maryanne.

Her two grandparents were both in their late seventies and refused to take on the care of her siblings. She talked to social workers, and thought of everything that she could do, but nothing worked out. A foster home wouldn't take her crippled sister, and her brother became hysterical at the thought of leaving home and living with strangers.

It turned out that she had no choice but to take care of them herself, but where? Her home in New York was only a one-bedroom apartment, and she needed to have three bedrooms, which she knew she could not afford. If she moved back home, the siblings' lives would be better, as their friends and schools were there, but she would then have to find a job in the nearest city, which was Omaha, Nebraska. It would be a good hour commute. If she kept her job in New York, she would also have to have a long commute in order to have an apartment that was reasonable enough for her to afford. What would happen to her relationship with Andrew? Would he want to take on that new burden with her? She didn't think so.

Her company was giving her time off because of the death of her family, but it couldn't be a long leave of absence. Instead of facing all her choices, she went into a state of deep depression. Her friends and Andrew tried to help her, but she wouldn't even talk with them. Finally, Andrew flew out to be with her. He saw the situation and the state she was in and comforted her by trying to help her be more positive. This was not the end of the world, the end of her job, or the end of their relationship. He was there to help her, and he did.

The first thing he did was find a convalescent home for Maryanne's sister that was paid for by the state. She needed to do rehabilitation and go back to school. They had the facilities for all of that. He saw that the sister was also depressed, so he coached her into believing that everything would be all right. The rehabilitation treatments would help her to walk someday, and she would have a normal life.

He gently approached her brother, Steve. Andrew slowly befriended Steve and got him talking. Andrew finally asked him about his desires and what he would like to see happen. After a while, Steve revealed to Andrew his hopes about going to college. He had never told anyone, but he really admired Maryanne and wanted to do as well as she had. No one in the family, especially his parents, had ever been interested in him, but he really wanted to apply to a college in Omaha. His grades were good, and Steve said that his teachers felt he would be eligible for some scholarships. He didn't want to go to a foster home. He wanted to finish his school years at home. The parents of one of Steve's closest friends had offered to take him in to finish high school. Andrew went and talked with them and made the arrangements for that to happen.

Andrew also looked at the finances. There wasn't much, but the house was worth some money, so he arranged to sell that and divide the money between the two younger siblings. They needed it more than Maryanne.

By this time, Maryanne was starting to feel positive and much better. Andrew told her that when they got married, they would find a bigger place with two or three bedrooms, so that when her sister had recovered from rehabilitation, she could live with them and go to private school if need be. He had a good job, and between the two of them, they could pay for it. Her sister would be finished with school in three years and then could go to college or do something else on her own. Then they would consider starting their own family.

In a short time, it was all arranged and they flew home together.

This story really shows the power of positive thinking. Fortunately, Maryanne had a man who wouldn't let her succumb to her darkest moods. If she had been positive, she could have made the same arrangements, but her negativity kept her from seeing what was possible. Her brother couldn't even talk with her because she was in such a dark place, and her sister felt like a huge burden when she didn't have to feel that way. Everything worked out as arranged. Her brother graduated from college with honors and continued on to receive an MBA in business. Her sister also excelled in private school and went on to college and a good career in advertising.

Sometimes, when a person gets into a negative place, she can't see the rainbow through the clouds. When the clouds become too heavy, the rain keeps pouring down without any hope of clearing. If you ever feel such depression, remember that there is a rainbow above, waiting for you to see and experience it.

The heart is the only way to move through the clouds. It has the ability to cut through the darkness and help you find the light. Sometimes what seems impossible is just an illusion. A teacher of mine once said to me, "The impossible just takes a little longer."

All of life has its ups and downs. Positive thinking and the use of the heart is always the way to tackle any obstacle. It is through the obstacles that a person grows. If life were always wonderful, it would bring no challenges, and if you had no challenges, then you would have a boring life and lose the chance to go through changes. It is changes that help you not only understand yourself more but also to look at life differently. If you see life through rose-colored glasses, you only see a certain segment of life, and this keeps you from experiencing all of it, both the positive and negative. It's good to see the negatives as learning posts that keep you moving forward.

Exercise:

Make a list of all the challenges you have had in the past year. Rate them according to which were the most difficult to face. Then, taking each one, ask yourself the following questions:
How did I handle this challenge?
What did I need to learn from it?
Was its resolution a right one?
Is it a challenge that I feel I won?
Is it a challenge that I feel I lost?
If I lost it, do I feel it will come up again in my life?
If that happens, how will I handle it differently?
If I won it, do I feel it will come up again in my life?
If that happens, will I handle it the same way or will I change the way in which I handle it?
When I again look at this challenge, was it a challenge I now realize was good for me to go through?

Often a person goes through a challenge, or what she considers an obstacle, and doesn't understand why she had to go through it or how important it was to have been confronted with it in the first place. With each challenge, there is a big question of the best way to handle it. Sometimes a person will face the challenge and boldly confront it and change it, but many people will become depressed or even feel that this shouldn't be happening to them. Realize that every challenge is meant to happen to you. It's like the old saying, "Do you see the glass half full or half empty?"

See challenges as ways to understand yourself, and most of all, as ways to understand the areas in your life that need changing. Such opportunities seldom come to a person because challenges are avoided and not really seen in the proper manner. The following story is an example of this:

> Jonathan was married with two children. He lived with his family in a rural area near New York City, where he worked for a financial firm on Wall Street. His life was very simple. He commuted every day to his office and read the newspaper on the train. His was a very typical life. Jonathan loved his wife and children, and they had good friends with whom they socialized.
>
> One day while riding the train to work, a beautiful young woman sat down next to him, and soon they were in a deep discussion concerning world events. Sharon was her name, and when they parted at the train station, they exchanged business cards. When Sharon called him a couple of days later, he felt very happy. They arranged to have a quick drink after work before going home. Sharon was also married, lived in a nearby town, and picked up the train at a later station.
>
> Soon their meetings became longer and longer, and they both told their partners that they were working late. The relationship progressed to an affair. They rented a motel in another town near them on weekend afternoons and made up excuses to their partners. It became a huge challenge for both of them to maintain their marriages, and soon they were talking of separating with their spouses to be together more permanently.
>
> In the meantime, Jonathan's wife, Mildred, started to pick up that something was happening, and one day,

she followed him to where he was meeting Sharon. When she confronted him, he told her the truth and asked her for a divorce. Sharon also told her husband, Roger, about her affair. Roger told a friend who knew Jonathan, and soon rumors were circulating throughout the two communities.

Mildred asked Jonathan to leave, so he temporarily rented a small apartment in town. Roger refused to let Sharon leave and begged her to go to counseling with him. She agreed, and they both started to work out the problems in their marriage, which made her decide to give it another try.

Jonathan was very disappointed when she told him this, particularly since he had gone the whole route and had left Mildred. He suddenly was left with no one and could only see his children every other weekend. He became very depressed and unhappy. His job was an important one, and he did his best to hide his feelings, but his work started to suffer. Finally, his boss talked with him and asked him what was the matter. When Jonathan told him, the boss insisted that he go into therapy.

His therapist helped him to see that having an affair in the first place was a result of something happening in the marriage and that maybe the first thing he needed to do was look at what that was. He realized that he had lost touch with his family. His life had seemed fine, but when he looked more deeply at his feelings, he understood how false that had been. He had provided for everyone, was a pleaser, and did what his wife and children wanted, but in actuality, he had never expressed his needs in the relationship. It was a life in which he participated, but he had never wanted it fully.

He soon realized that he hated living in a rural place and that his true love was the city, so he found himself a small apartment in Greenwich Village and fixed it up according to his own tastes. His home had always been taken care of and decorated by his wife. In fact, she always arranged their whole social life, and he had gone along with it. He also decided to take some night courses and study painting, a hobby that he had loved when he was much younger. His apartment was arranged so that he had a corner of the living area sectioned off for his painting materials.

Not only did his mood change as he changed his lifestyle, but his relationship with his children also became better. When they came to New York, he met them at the station and took them to all the museums and interesting places that the city had to offer. They loved it and wanted to see him more often, but he stayed firm about only seeing them every other weekend. He also started having them stay with him during some of their school vacations.

Fortunately, his earnings were enough that he did not have too much of a financial setback, and even though his relationship with Sharon had not worked, he now had a much better lifestyle than the one he had lived with for so long.

The divorce went through, and Mildred started to work in her previous career as a schoolteacher. She also was starting to feel much happier, and she and Jonathan stayed friends. Their lives had changed for the better, and both eventually remarried. Even though the obstacles they had to go through seemed huge at the time, the outcome was much better for both of them.

When someone like Jonathan goes through obstacles that seem unsolvable at the time, the heart connection is lost, and then a person can plunge into deep doldrums and not see a clear way out. Fortunately, Jonathan listened to his boss and went into therapy, and the therapist helped him to refocus on his heart's needs. Connecting again with his heart and his real feelings helped him to look at the positive part of the whole situation. He then could find for himself what truly made him happy and in so doing, start the lifestyle that he needed to flourish.

Exercise:

Ask your Higher Self the following questions:

*When I go through a challenge or obstacle, do I try to be
in my heart and understand it better?*
*If it is a challenge that I feel is impossible to resolve, do
I seek help?*
*Do challenges and obstacles generally put me in a nega-
tive mood?*
*If the answer is yes, ask: Do I try to change my mood
right away?*
*When I look back on what I went through, am I able to
see all the ramifications clearly?*
Do I remember to be in my heart?

Remember that life itself will bring you challenges that seem too difficult to handle. If you look at these as ways to grow and bring change into
your life, then you can more easily reconnect to your heart and use your
heart in the process of resolving them. There is very little in life that can't
be solved. The worst situations can be resolved, even if they take a little
longer.

The heart is a beautiful instrument that gives you strength, wisdom and
positive energy. Remember, it can always help you in the worst of times.

21

Using the Heart to Handle People's Reactions

When you are talking with someone and he reacts badly to your words, how do you handle it? If he becomes angry or upset and reacts with negative emotions, what do you do? A person may take something you said the wrong way, or even become confused by what you said.

Clarity in speaking, particularly when the subject has emotions attached to it, can be difficult. A good example would be telling a loved one he has done something you feel unhappy about. The loved one may react by becoming defensive, and then you, in turn, become defensive. Then an argument can start over what you said. It's important to try not to become defensive, but, instead, to link with your heart and speak the right words to calm the situation. This is what is meant by using your heart to handle people's reactions. When it comes to emotions, it can be very difficult not to react. Even when the emotions are positive, there can be reactions that are too much to handle calmly. If you use your heart, it will always clear the emotions and leave you with a deeper understanding of what needs to happen and the proper words to use. Too often, reactions are so strong that the proper way to proceed is lost.

Exercise:

> *Ask yourself the following questions:*
> *When someone reacts to my words in a negative manner, how do I handle it?*

When someone reacts to my words in an overly positive manner, how do I handle it?

Do I have different feelings when a loved one reacts to my words compared to when someone who is simply a friend reacts to them?

If the answer to this is yes, ask: What is the difference and how does it make me feel?

Can I remain calm and in my heart when I get into an argument?

How do I behave when I am part of a group of people reacting to each other?

If I am leading a group and the group starts to argue, how do I handle it?

If I am talking with a child or teenager and he strongly reacts, how do I handle it?

Am I aware when I am speaking in a way that can be upsetting to a person?

If I am aware, do I try to change my way of speaking?

If I am not aware and the person I am talking with tells me that he is upset with how I sound, what is my reaction?

When I need to speak with someone about a difficult situation, do I try to be kind and in my heart when I speak with him?

Unfortunately, most people are not aware of how their voice sounds when they confront someone, or even when they are talking normally. A person may feel his words are fine, when in fact the tone of his voice may sound harsh. It's important to always point this out to the person as he may not know the way he sounds, or he may be feeling a certain way and his tone of voice is conveying it, but he is not aware that he is doing it. It's difficult to become more conscious of how you sound to others.

People who have a leadership role in this life, or have had one in a past life, can sound very authoritarian and not realize it. Such behavior can be completely unconscious, and if you tell the person that you are hearing this in the tone of his voice, he may disagree and have a negative reaction to your criticism. The way to change this is always to remember to be in your heart when you talk with someone, but it takes practice to overcome an ingrained habit.

The following is a story that illustrates this:

Jenny was a difficult woman who had very few friends because most people felt she was bossy and not very pleasant. When a friend pointed this out to her, she totally disagreed and claimed the friend was projecting onto her. She said the friend was the authoritarian one. This did not fit the friend, who then also backed away from the relationship.

Jenny was in her late twenties and had several affairs with men who always broke up with her, mainly because they didn't care for her superior manner. One man told her this, but she did not believe him and, again, felt it was all a projection on his part.

One day she was walking down the street of her hometown and bumped into Ralph, an old boyfriend from her late teens. They greeted each other and he asked her to have coffee with him to catch up. When they sat down, he started the conversation by asking, "How have you been? What's happening in your life?"

She responded by telling him about her job and, in turn, asked him what he was doing.

"I'm actually searching to change careers. I'm working for a corporation that I feel is way behind the times, and even though it's a good job and pays well, I would like to be in a company that is looking more to the future. I just got my MBA and need to apply it more in the work I'm doing."

They talked some more about their companies, and Jenny suggested he apply for a job in her corporation, as they were looking for someone who had his background.

They didn't talk about their personal lives except to say that neither one of them was married.

Ralph was delighted with the job offer he later received from her corporation and felt the new job was just what he was looking for. Jenny was in a managerial position, and Ralph was hired in another branch, also as a manager, and even though they didn't work together, sometimes their projects were similar enough that information could be shared between the two branches.

Ralph's boss didn't know that he had gotten the job through a recommendation from Jenny. When Ralph spoke with his supervisor and was told he needed to sometimes exchange information with Jenny's group, his boss said, "Be careful in your dealings with Jenny. She can be really difficult to work with." The boss explained that she had a reputation of acting authoritative and not too many people liked her.

Ralph asked, "But if that is the case, why hasn't she been fired or at least told about this?"

"She has been told, but, unfortunately, she doesn't believe it and lays the blame on others," said Ralph's boss. "Her work is excellent, so there is no way her boss would let her go. Her staff just puts up with it because they can learn a lot from her. It's a sad story."

Ralph thought about this and decided that he needed, in some way, to help Jenny realize that her personality was making her disliked.

He started by asking her to occasionally have lunch with him, and soon he saw that she overpowered the conversation and that she was very opinionated. He would sometimes interject a comment to change the subject, but she ignored it and continued talking about what she saw or thought about a situation, which spanned the gauntlet from national to corporate politics. He always found her attractive but very rigid.

He decided to ask her to dinner one night and bought her a couple of strong drinks, with the hope that she would be more relaxed. His memory of her as a teen was that she was very quiet and nice. Something must have happened to change her, and that's what he started to ask about: what was her romantic story since then?

She was reluctant to talk about it, so he started sharing his past and some of the hurts he had gone through with the hope that she would do the same.

She, instead, started to give her opinion of what he had done wrong.

Finally, he interrupted her and said, "I was sharing what happened to me, not asking what I could have done to change it. I was simply sharing, and it would be nice to hear some of your stories. I promise not to be judgmental in any way. I hope we can be friends and do that."

Jenny looked at him and became silent. Her eyes looked thoughtful. "I'm not used to sharing anything. I like to analyze, not share."

"Is sharing painful for you?"

"Well, I think that is very feminine, and I'm not into being like that. I need to know what's happening at all times."

"It sounds like you need to be in control of what is happening to you in order to be safe. Why is that?"

"It's more than feeling safe, though I guess that is part of it. I never thought about that before. It's more about not having anyone treat me condescendingly."

"Did that happen in your family?"

"Yes, my father always treated my mother like that, and she never did a thing to stand up to him. I never want to be like her."

"It sounds like you are more like your father instead."

"No, of course not." The conversation ended after that.

It was the beginning. Slowly, Ralph was able to get Jenny to express her feelings more. She was terrified of being controlled by anyone, and to make sure that it would never happen, she had developed a strong negative personality that resembled her father's. She began thinking about what Ralph had said.

He never mentioned that she was authoritarian and controlling, never mentioned how her personality was disliked by others, but she was smart enough to realize that people didn't like her, and she remembered that she had been told something to that effect by her superior, which she had rejected at the time.

Ralph's approach was from his heart, gentle and nudging, and she realized he was much more feminine in some ways then she was. She also saw him operate in the office, where he was direct, kind, and considerate, and also accomplished his work very professionally. Mainly she saw how well liked he was. Maybe she should try to be more like him, she thought.

One day when they were having lunch, Jenny asked him, "Ralph, you are a man, very much so, but you also have a positive feminine part that is very nice to see. How did you develop that?"

He smiled, "Well, fortunately, I have a mother who has developed both. She was loving and nurturing and also strong and sensible. She shared a life with my father and he accepted her as his equal. It was a good growing up experience, so I was lucky. It sounds like you never had that from either parent, but it doesn't mean you can't develop it now. It's about opening your heart and believing that heart energy can be strong and not weak."

He went on to explain more about the way the heart operated.

Jenny thanked him and asked him to help her, which he slowly did. There were many times when she resisted, but he pushed through the resistance and she began to feel the difference and the change in herself. Her mannerism became softer. She listened to her staff instead of always telling them what to do, and she also tried to listen to the tone of her voice. People started to notice the change in her and became friendlier with her. She was even invited to a couple of parties and really enjoyed herself, being careful to listen and not command attention.

She and Ralph became close friends and confided in each other. Their relationship was never romantic, which they both agreed might hurt the good friendship they had together. Eventually, both found partners and

married, and when Jenny took a leave of absence to
have a child, the office threw her a big party. She now
had the tools to become a positive, loving mother.

When someone has a balance of the feminine and masculine qualities, it can be a man, like in Ralph's case, or a woman. These qualities have
nothing to do with gender, but sometimes are associated with gender. The
feminine qualities mainly work with the heart and help the heart to express
itself to others in a gentle, loving way. That is why it is important to work
with your heart on a daily basis whether you are a woman or a man. If you
are in your heart, you will always speak in a calm, clear and sometimes
loving manner. If, for example, you need to give direction to someone who
doesn't listen well, being in your heart will help the information come out
in a direct manner–commanding in a gentle way, clear, but not demanding.

Sometimes a person does not need a loving response, but, instead, needs
a more direct response. The heart knows which is best for that person.

The mistake is that some people feel it's important to always be sweet
and kind, but that may not be what's best for the person. It's important to realize that you can be direct, concise, and clear and still have it come from your
heart in the manner the person needs to hear it in order for it to have the right
effect. What never works is giving advice in a controlling or authoritarian
tone of voice. When that happens, the person immediately turns off.

Exercise:

*Think of a recent situation in which you had to be
directive with someone. Close your eyes and relive the
situation. Notice your tone of voice, and also notice the
manner in which you spoke with the person. Open your
eyes and ask yourself the following questions:*

Did I use the right tone of voice with this person?

When I spoke, was I clear and concise?

*Were there any controlling mannerisms in the way I
spoke?*

*Was I too laid back and kind when I shouldn't have
been?*

*Were my words easy for the person to hear and under-
stand?*

*Did I feel my message was heard and accepted by the
person?*

Did I express what I needed to say?

Did I link with my heart before talking?
Did I feel it was a successful conversation?
If the answer is no, ask: What went wrong?
Do I need to follow up with this person another time?

If you feel from answering the questions that you needed to do more or speak differently, do the following:

Exercise:

Close your eyes, link with your heart, and again re-
live the same scene but change how you talk with the
person, incorporating some of the things you have just
learned. Open your eyes and ask yourself the following
questions:
How did that feel?
Was the response from the person different?
Do I feel my message was heard?
Was the outcome different?
Did I feel that my words were fully expressed?
Did I in any way feel I failed in this scenario?
If the answer is yes, ask: What caused the failure?

If for some reason you failed to convey the message clearly and correctly, redo the scene and try to rectify the outcome. Then ask yourself the same preceding questions.

When you feel you have done this scene with an open heart and can redo it with the same positive outcome, close your eyes to replay the scene.

This time you will be above the scene, looking down
at yourself and the person, and you will be observing
all that is happening from above. Listen to the tone of
your voice and the other person's voice. Notice the body
movements. Observe how your words are affecting the
person. Get a deeper understanding about the whole
scenario.
Then open your eyes and ask yourself the following
questions:
How did that feel to observe myself and the other per-
son?

> *Did I notice something in my tone of voice that I hadn't noticed before?*
> *Did I notice something in the body movements that I hadn't noticed before?*
> *When I observed the other person, was there something in his attitude that wasn't clear before?*
> *Do I still feel that this has a positive outcome, or is something still missing?*
> *If the answer is yes, something is missing, ask: What is missing?*

It's always good to do this kind of exercise when you are thinking about something that happened in the past that you want to understand better. Particularly when you are the observer from above, it brings a new perspective to the situation.

How we sound to others can cause misunderstandings or the opposite—make your relationships clear and unclouded. Often a person thinks he is conveying what is necessary, but in actuality he has not made himself clear. When misunderstanding arises, it's good to go back and try to understand what got lost in the communication. If for any reason you are not clear about what was really being said to you, it's important to tell the person that you do not understand and ask him to please explain what he means more clearly. You can do this in a nice way, without making the person feel you are criticizing him. Misunderstood communication is extremely common. If nothing is said, then the information can become even more distorted when it is repeated.

Exercise:

> *Ask your Higher Self the following questions:*
> *Do I always express myself clearly?*
> *If the answer is no, ask: How can I be more aware when I am unclear?*
> *If I don't understand what someone is saying to me, do I tell the person this?*
> *If the answer is no, ask: Why don't I do this?*
> *If I am in a group of people talking and the conversation gets carried away in a direction I don't understand, do I ask for someone to explain it to me?*
> *If the answer is no, ask: Why not?*

*Have I been involved in several misunderstandings in
the past year?
If the answer is yes, go over them and look at your part
in making them happen.
Have I answered all the above questions correctly?*

In the future, when you have a difficult conversation with someone, go over the above exercises and try to determine, first, what your tone of voice was, and then, if you conveyed the message you wanted to convey in a clear, concise, and sometimes loving, manner. Ask if you remembered to link with your heart.

It's important to remember that every conversation can end in a positive manner, even when it is one that is more directive. It takes practice to start to hear yourself talk. If there are several people in the conversation, ask one of them with whom you are close if he felt you spoke in a clear and nice manner. Even ask the person how you sounded to him, especially if it is someone you know well, and definitely if you felt uncertain about how you conveyed the message. Your friends will tell you when they feel you are not clear or positive, particularly if you tell them you are working on this.

Basically, it is very important to be in your heart at all times. Then you will respond in a positive manner. Being in your heart is the key.

22

Integrating the Use of the Heart into the Whole Person

When a person uses her heart on a regular basis, it will change the person in many ways. First of all, the person will feel different, especially if the person had been mostly using her mind and was active in the world using more masculine energy.

When the heart is functioning, it changes not only the outward behavior of an individual, but it also changes the way a person operates. What I mean is that the person becomes more intuitive and more inward in her thinking. For example, if you are someone who responds to a situation right away and goes into action to resolve things, that is using more of the mind and masculine energy. If you begin to use your heart more, you will think about the situation first and even go into a feeling mode before acting. This is working with both the mind and the heart before responding.

This type of response leads to a better outcome and it also deepens the way something is done, whereas immediate action can create a disturbance and may not necessarily be the right action. This, of course, does not include responding to a sudden emergency, which has to be done immediately.

Sometimes, when a mind-oriented person starts to use her heart, it not only feels difficult and strange, but also it can make the person feel she isn't responding quickly enough. In some cases that may be true, especially if the person spends too much time contemplating what to do.

At first it may be difficult for you, so it's best to experiment with every situation. Notice how long you take when you use your heart, and also notice if the feeling is uncomfortable for you. There are ways in which to gradually start to work with your heart that will not be disturbing, especially if you are someone who hasn't consciously done this before.

Some of the ways are the following:

Exercise:

> *Put the information about a situation into your heart for a minute or two, not longer. Then take any result from that and think about it. Next, take that thought and put it into your heart and go deeper with that thought. Do this several times until you decide on the right action.*
>
> *Ask yourself first if you need to make a quick decision about this, or if you have time to do the process described above.*
>
> *When a decision has to be made and you have some time, try taking time to think about it. Come up with a final conclusion, then put it into your heart and check the response your heart has when you say this is the right solution. If you feel a lack of warmth or movement, then the solution is not the right one. Then try working with the solution by doing the process in step one.*
>
> *Next, take a problem you have already solved where you felt dissatisfied by the outcome, put that into your heart and ask: What would have been a better solution to this problem?*
>
> *Check the answer you received from your mind by putting the answer into your heart and asking if it was correct. Again, your heart will respond or not respond. If it doesn't respond, try feeling the answer coming from your heart.*
>
> *If you are a mind person and have difficulty using your heart, ask your Higher Self the following questions:*
> *Do I have any fears around using my heart more?*

If the answer is yes, ask what the fears are.
Did something happen in my childhood that keeps me
from using my heart?
If the answer is yes, ask what happened.
Was I born with the tendency to be more mind ori-
ented?
If the answer is yes, ask what that comes from.
Taking the answers from the above questions, ask for a
process and a first step in changing each one.

Using the heart can bring up fears related to love, since most people feel that is the main function of the heart. As the previous chapters explain, the heart's function is much more complex; giving and receiving personal love is just a small part of it. But if there are blocks concerning love, it can interfere with developing the heart center.

The following story illustrates this:

> Marvin was a very successful man who lived in a large town near a major city. His business took him back and forth between the town and the city, an hour drive each way. In his late twenties, he was in a major accident on the highway. It left him crippled and in a wheelchair for life.
>
> At the time, he was single but engaged to be married. When he realized he would not walk again, he broke his engagement, telling his fiancé that he did not want her to have to take care of him and that he would get help and be better off living alone. Sally, his fiancé, protested, but he refused to talk with her about it, so finally she gave up and left.
>
> His business was ruined because he could no longer commute back and forth, which was a necessary part of the job. Instead, he decided to start a home business that he could run on his computer. He became an online consultant in his field, which was related to medicine and medical research. Part of his previous job was to go to doctors to push the brands of his company. Now he consulted with several pharmaceutical companies and introduced new products to a range of practitioners, and even some research-

ers who were looking for certain chemicals informing
them about some of the newest research studies. It was
a good business, and he was easily able to have enough
money for therapists to work on his legs and for someone to cook and clean his house and do errands.

Marvin's life was simple. He had a few friends who
visited him once in a while, but he was alone most of
the time. He never complained, but accepted that this
was the way he would have to live the rest of his life.
Only once in a while did he think about Sally and what
it would have been like to be married to her and to
have a family of his own.

In the beginning there was hope that eventually,
with therapy, he could bring his legs back enough to
use a walker, but that wasn't happening. He kept doing the therapy simply because he needed to maintain
good circulation so he wouldn't get any blood clots.

After three or four years of this, his therapist said
that she was leaving to move to the city, but she had a
good replacement who would come with her a couple
of times to learn the procedure. Janet, the new woman,
was in her mid-twenties, young and very beautiful.
Marvin immediately felt upset that she was to be the
new therapist. She brought up his longing for his ex-
fiancé. Janet even reminded him of Sally in the way
she looked and spoke. She was very professional and
seemed to be a good therapist. She also felt that other
methods the previous therapist hadn't tried might activate his legs. Marvin felt very confused. He wanted her
to stay and do the new methods, but it broke his heart
every time he looked at her. He decided that in order
to keep her, he had to shut down any feelings he had.

Janet was very heart-oriented, and when Marvin
started shutting down emotionally, she felt it right
away. Finally, after a couple of weeks of this, she
confronted him and asked him why he was no longer
responding to her but had distanced himself. She asked
him to tell her if she had done something to cause this,
as she was concerned about doing a good job.

He reluctantly told her what the problem was and also told her about his broken engagement to Sally. She encouraged him to call Sally and see her again. He followed her advice, and Sally came to see him. They both cried when they saw each other. Sally had been dating, but she had never forgotten him and wanted to be with him. By this time, the work with Janet had helped renew some of the nerves in his legs, and he was beginning to walk with a walker. When Sally came back into his life, he became happy again and felt his heart reopen.

When the heart is fully functioning, it makes a person more whole. This means that the heart affects everything someone does. For example, if you are working on a project and the project requires both your mental and your analytical skills and you don't connect to your heart for inspiration, then you are not using your full potential. Using your heart takes skill and concentration, but it will help a person achieve her goals and be successful in any enterprise she undertakes.

Wholeness is also about balance within and without. The heart knows what is lacking in an individual and the best way to handle any situation. If you are uncertain on how to proceed, even if you have the skill to make something work, by checking with your heart you will have a better indication of the best method to continue. The balance between the heart and mind is very important, and when it becomes imbalanced, a person can get stuck and take the wrong direction. Too often someone looks at a project and chooses how to proceed because of previous experiences. This can be a good method, but it may not necessarily have a positive outcome, particularly if other people are involved. A good example is the following story:

Jacob was a very busy, active man in charge of sales for a company he co-owned with a friend. The business was doing very well, but the economy had gone into a slow period and sales went down. Previously, he would wait it out and not worry, as sales usually went up and down. This time, however, he found that six months later the sales continued to be down, something he hadn't foreseen because of his previous experience. He and his partner conferred and his partner came up with an idea to add to their inventory and take on some other related products that still seemed to be selling. They did this and, almost immediately, sales went up.

Jacob would never have come up with this idea on his own, as he was set in his old way of thinking. He was functioning in a limited way. But if he had taken time to put the whole picture into his heart, the inspiration would have come through about expanding their product line.

Most successful entrepreneurs work with their hearts. They never feel stuck in one methodology and are able to expand their viewpoint to include more solutions.

Another example is someone who is given a plan to follow and sticks faithfully to the plan, never allowing creativity to come in when the plan isn't working well. Creativity is a key to using the heart. The heart not only inspires a person, but it also gives one creative methods to follow through. If, for example, you are given a project to accomplish and you put it into your heart, asking for the best method to follow through, you may find yourself thinking about something that is entirely new. Or, you may think about a method that you have used before, but add to it the idea to plan it out in a better way. The heart opens every possibility.

Integrating the use of your heart means using it in everything you do, whether it is working on a personal problem or something larger. To start to do this consciously can prove difficult, especially if you are more mind-oriented. For example, if you want to use your heart all day long, it takes concentration to remember to do this. You need determination and focus to make it happen. You can link with your heart initially when starting something, but then you can easily forget and continue the work solely in your mind. Most of the steps that this book has given you so far can certainly help you to focus on the heart, but you also need an inner knowledge that doing the work helps make you more whole as a person. Let's look at what I mean by wholeness.

- You try to use your heart and mind in your work and in your relationships.

- When you finish something, you feel you have done the best that you could.

- You are able to accept your faults and, at the same time, accept your strong points.
- You do not need outside approval for who you are.
- You are content with yourself, from the way you look to how you relate to others.
- You know that certain things can improve, but you are not a perfectionist and you realize that nothing in life is perfect.
- You are able to work with others and not feel competitive.
- You sincerely enjoy other people's work, even when they have more skills than you.
- If you don't understand or know something, you are not afraid to ask for advice and help.
- You are not critical of others or yourself.
- You genuinely like who you are.
- When you see you are lacking in something, you try to change it.
- If you feel negative, you try to change your thoughts to being more positive.
- You are open to new solutions.
- You welcome feedback on your projects.
- You can step back and look at a situation or problem in a disidentifed manner.
- You enjoy life and try to make your life full of adventure and fun.
- You love the people you are close to and don't have any expectations of them.
- Generally, you see the glass half full, not half empty.
- When you look back at your life, you can mostly accept the manner in which you lived it.
- If you have regrets about anything you have done, you don't hold onto them but instead learn from them.
- When you look to the future, you feel there is still more to learn and look forward to.

Exercise:

> You may agree or disagree with some of the above con-
> cepts as to what constitutes a whole being. Take the list,
> change it, and even add to it so that what you have is
> a goal toward which you would like to work. Take your
> final list and prioritize it, putting at the top the thing
> you would like to work on first. Then take the top item
> and ask your Higher Self the following questions:
> How can I start to work on achieving this? Give me a
> process and a first step.
> Is there anything blocking me from doing this?
> If the answer is yes, ask what it is.
> Then ask: How can I overcome this block?

This exercise can take a while to do, particularly if you add to your list. Do not rush it. Try to work on only one item at a time until you feel you have achieved most of it. Sometimes you may find that when you work on one item, it starts to relate to another. If this is the case, include the second one in the work.

Try to use your heart when you do this work, as the use of your heart will help you become more integrated and able to work through the difficulties that arise in your daily life. Your heart has a deeper understanding of what you need to do to succeed, and it certainly will bring you closer to others. The mind's function is also positive, but without the use of your heart, it will cause an imbalance and lead you away from wholeness.

23

It's Okay to Not Always Be Connected to the Heart

When you work with your heart on a regular basis, you may find that sometimes it is very fatiguing. The reason for this is that it's like learning a new instrument that hasn't been tuned yet. There will be times when the instrument doesn't sound right, and also times when your practice isn't going well, and you choose to put the instrument down for a while so that when you return to it, it will be fresh and invigorating.

The same is true when working with the heart. All of the exercises in this book should be done slowly, and if a certain exercise is too difficult for you to do, then leave it and come back to it when you feel more confident that you are ready to tackle it. A lot of this work relates to inner processes, and sometimes a person will not be in the proper mood to do such work.

A good example is someone who is attending school. Your heart will always help you, but you may find yourself in a place where you simply have to be in the mind to study and learn specific knowledge. This is all analytical work and needs deep mental concentration. Only when the work requires something that is creative and imaginative should your heart be brought into the work. Certainly, if you are fatigued and feel overwhelmed, you should use your heart to bring yourself more balance. But, if the fatigue is from overwork, you may simply have to take a nap to recoup. Let's look at some ways you can recognize when you needn't do the heart work:

- When you are negative or irritated and need to change your mood by doing something physical, like hitting a pillow or going for a long walk in nature.
- When you are working on a plan of action that requires physical movement, such as competing in a contest like running a marathon.
- When you feel very tired and just need to rest.
- When you feel ill and need to sleep and renew your body.
- When you are doing any physical labor, such as cleaning the house or doing heavy lifting.
- When you are talking to a professional about some kind of policy you own.
- When you are talking to a lawyer or an accountant about specific work to be done.
- Sometimes you simply can't work further with your heart because you have been concentrating on the heart a long time and feel it is too much.
- When your job requires you to take transportation and you are concentrating on getting some place by following written directions.
- When you are driving and need to be alert to traffic conditions.
- When you have to be in charge of a group of people and help them find where they need to go.
- When you need to relax, read a book, or play a mental game.
- When you have to prepare food and you are following a recipe.
- When you feel scattered and need to focus more on a task.
- When you feel too emotional to connect to your heart.
- When you are in a conversation that is based on specific information.
- When you have the need to isolate yourself and not talk with anyone, and being in your heart may take away that need.

- When you are visiting a friend who is ill and you need to help him in practical ways.

- When you are working on an analytical project and need to supply the written data.

- When you are engaged in any work that is based on information or data already supplied. But the use of your heart comes in when you need to develop your own data.

The main thing to look for is when you feel overwhelmed by the heart work. As you develop your instrument, it will become easier to play, but in the developmental stages you can overdo it.

Exercise:

> *Ask yourself the following questions:*
> *What signs do I have that show when I may be overdoing the heart work?*
> *Do I have any fears in doing this work, fears that make me feel too tired?*
> *How can I best determine when I should not be working with the heart?*
> *When I take a break from the work, what should I be doing?*
> *How will I know if not doing the heart work is correct?*
> *Is there some part of the work that is causing me difficulties?*
> *If the answer is yes, ask: What is it?*
> *What is my feeling when I stop working with the heart for a while?*
> *If I need to recoup, how long should I take a break?*

After you have answered the above questions, check out your answers with your Higher Self. Particularly, be certain about how long of a break you should take. If the answer is more than three days, question it. Your lower nature may try to interfere with you on this.

The following story illustrates this:

> Stewart was a quiet, reserved, middle-aged man with a wife and two grown up children. He and his wife, Jennifer, lived in the suburbs and they both worked, commuting to a city nearby. Stewart was in

the real estate business in the city, and he also had to work weekends, as he sold condos as well as commercial real estate. It was a very lucrative business, and he and Jennifer were able to save a lot of their income for their retirement. Jennifer worked for a corporation as a manager, also making a good salary.

They both felt very happy in the marriage and through the years had settled any differences. Basically, they had the same goal, to retire in the countryside, where they had a small house that they used on weekends. Their plans were to eventually tear down that house and build a larger one to accommodate their children's families when they visited them.

One day when Stewart was working in the city, he suffered a stroke and unfortunately lost the use of his left side. He never fully recovered and, therefore, had to quit his job, which was a blow to both of them and their plans. It meant that Jennifer was now the main breadwinner of the family. She made enough for them to live on, but not enough for them to continue saving for their retirement.

Stewart, while he was convalescing, received a book from a friend on working with the heart. He started to practice doing this, as he thought that maybe it would help him be more creative in developing an alternate plan so they still could have their home in the country. He was very focused from his many years of working in real estate, and he used this ability to do the exercises and develop his heart and creativity. He loved the work and practiced rigorously for several hours every day while Jennifer was at work. But every night when Jennifer came home, he was exhausted and could barely talk with her. He believed this had to do with his condition, as did she. He went to bed early and slept in until help came to take care of him. Previously, they had shared everything, but Jennifer was also tired. She was now taking on all the chores of the household on top of working full time.

Stewart was spending his days working hard on using his heart to help develop a way to continue to do some work in order to bring in more money. He looked at their investments, which were handled by a broker, but his heart helped him realize it would be too risky to start fooling around with those. At least they were stable. Then he looked into selling their home in the suburbs and buying a condo instead. That would free up some money, which could then be added to their investments. Jennifer could not retire for ten years, however, and that would mean there would be no room for their children to come and visit.

When he spoke to Jennifer about it, she became very upset. He said the kids could always go to a hotel instead, and, besides, they could also visit the kids more when he became more mobile. This resulted in a big fight, something they hadn't had for many years. Stewart gave in and went back to trying constantly to work with his heart to discover a way to work toward their goal.

By this time, he was able to get around in a wheel-chair and had some mobility, not much, but enough to no longer need daytime help. He found he was becoming more and more tired, and when he tried working with his heart, he felt he just couldn't do it anymore. Basically, he gave up, stopped working with the heart, and stopped trying to come up with any new ideas. He spent his time reading books and sleeping.

In the meantime, Jennifer was tired also. It was affecting her job, and after a lot of discussion with her children, she decided to put Stewart into a nursing home. He had been a veteran, so he could stay in a VA home that would not cost them anything. She knew she had to do it, even if she didn't want to. Their life together no longer existed. Stewart didn't care either. He had lost all hope, and he only lived a couple of years in the VA home before he died.

Jennifer stayed in her home and retired there, and she basically stopped going to the country house. She

gave it to her children to use whenever they wanted.
She blamed their lost dreams on Stewart for having a
stroke.

This story could have ended another way. If Stewart had stayed positive and continued to work with his heart and his creativity, he would have come up with a way to make money by consulting on the computer. He had a very successful background in his field. He could also have done computer classes for people wanting to go into the business. His firm had even told him that when he was better, they could still use him to do research work. When he was better, he never bothered. By then he was too negative and was escaping by reading books. He also could have planned to rest more in the daytime so that he would be awake in the evenings and still share dinner and conversation with Jennifer. He overdid his work with developing the heart until he was so fatigued that it blocked anything he could do.

This is why it's important to work with this book slowly and to know that it is ongoing work that cannot be done in a short time. Even developing the heart a small amount will make a difference, and you will feel the difference.

Exercise:

> *Ask your Higher Self the following questions:*
> *Am I working with my heart in a balanced manner?*
> *If the answer is no, ask: What is not balanced?*
> *Do I know when I should take a rest from working with my heart?*
> *If the answer is no, ask: How can I know?*
> *When I work with my heart, am I always conscious of the energy I am using?*
> *If the answer is no, ask: How can I be more conscious of this?*
> *Is there a practice I can use to help me understand the most beneficial manner in which to work with my heart?*
> *If the answer is yes, ask: What is it?*
> *Is anything stopping me from being more balanced?*
> *If the answer is yes, ask: What is it?*

Basically, everything you practice should be in balance and not be too taxing; otherwise, you are overdoing it. We live in a society in which many people are working long hours, and these people often become workahol-ics. It is a way of life that can take a hard toll on a person. The opposite also exists, people who do very little work and expect to be taken care of.

Exercise:

> *Ask yourself if you are either one of these types of people. Are you a workaholic or indolent? If the answer is yes to one of those categories, ask yourself the follow-ing questions. (If you are neither, you need not do the exercise.)*
> *What caused me to become this way?*
> *Was it part of my childhood conditioning?*
> *Was there anyone in my family who was this way?*
> *If the answer is yes, ask: Do I in any way emulate this person?*
> *If you believe in past lives, ask your Higher Self: Did I bring this tendency over from a past life?*
> *Do I want to change this and become more balanced?*
> *If the answer is no, ask: Why do I want to hold onto this?*
> *If you want to change this, ask your Higher Self for a process and a first step.*

You may be surprised that a part of you does not want to change, that you are in a pattern that gives you something. If this is the case, then it's important to identify what you receive from holding onto this pattern.

Learning the proper way to work with the heart is a very personal pro-cess. How you work with it and how someone else does will vary com-pletely. There are as many ways to develop the heart as there are fish in the ocean. Don't carry too many expectations, and don't be self-critical or in any way feel you aren't doing enough. Some people can move through the exercises quickly, and others need to take more time. Just because you take longer and need more resting time, that doesn't mean you are not do-ing well. Just remembering some of the simple procedures, such as linking with your heart before doing anything, can be helpful. The heart is your instrument to learn how to play and to bring beauty to others. Its melody is your melody, unique and inspiring.

Part Six: Deepening the Experience

24

Looking at Your Goals in Life with the Heart

When you look at your goals in life with your heart, you may find that what you thought was a goal changes with the heart's energy. You may have several goals, so for now it is important to list them. For example, one goal may be to eventually retire and live in the country or it may be the opposite, you want to move from the suburbs and live in a big city. This would be a lifestyle goal.

Another goal might have to do with the work you do. You may want to become a major figure in the company where you work, or you may want to change jobs and work for a different type of company. This would be a work-related goal.

Another goal might concern relationships. You may be married with children, but in the future you may want to live alone and separate from that lifestyle, or you may be single and have the goal of being married or living with someone. This would be a relationship goal.

You may have a financial goal to have a certain amount of money saved for your retirement.

You may have a recreational goal, such as taking up painting, or using your leisure time to travel.

All of these may be goals and, of course, every one has many such aspects.

Exercise:

> *Make a list of all your goals. You may or may not want to put them under the categories I have mentioned, and you can add to them all legitimate goals. If, for example, you have a desire to learn how to play an instrument, you may put that down under work-related goals or you may put it under recreational goals. Set your list into a chart in which you can put some timelines. For example, you may do headings across the chart for each category or goal, and then list under those headings the various things you want to accomplish in that goal. Keep room under the headings for you to put a date by which you would like the goal to be completed. Then take the first category, such as Lifestyle Goals, and tackle each item under that heading. Put each in your heart and ask the following questions:*
>
> > *Is this goal realistic? Can I achieve it?*
> >
> > *If the answer is no, ask: What is not realistic about it?*
> >
> > *If it is unrealistic, ask: How can I change it so it is realistic?*
> >
> > *When I achieve this goal, how will it make me feel?*
> >
> > *If I don't achieve this goal, how will it make me feel?*
> >
> > *Is it possible that this goal should be worded differently and maybe even changed?*
> >
> > *If the answer is yes, ask: How should I do this?*
> >
> > *Where should this goal be placed in my prioritized list of goals under this category?*

In other words, you may start out with five goals under a category, but they are not necessarily in the right order of importance. You can redo this list and place them according to what your heart indicates.

This could end up as a big chart that you hang somewhere, or simply as individual pages with each goal on a separate page with a timeline. After you have completed all the categories, listed all the goals, and asked the above questions, you need to put them away and not look at them for at least a month. Then take them out again, and taking each category one at a time, read every goal under each category out loud.

Exercise:

> *Put all that you read concerning one category into your heart and ask your Higher Self:*
> *Do all of these goals under this category sound correct?*
> *If the answer is no, ask: Which one is not correct?*
> *Is there something missing under this category?*
> *If the answer is yes, ask: What is it?*
> *Is my timeline in achieving this correct?*
> *If the answer is no, ask: What is wrong with it?*
> *What is my first step in working toward achieving these goals?*
> *Is there anything that could change in my life to change these goals?*
> *If the answer is yes, ask: What is it?*

After you have done this with each category, take the list of goals under that category, close your eyes and see it all happening. In other words, if your goal is living in the country and having a home there, envision yourself in the country; imagine where it is and try to visualize the house and who is with you there. Make it all possible in your vision, and, finally, take that whole experience and put it into your heart and feel if it is right, or if something is wrong or missing. When you put it into your heart, it should feel right and you should feel warmth. If you don't, it is not really right for you. Do this with each category, and I suggest doing each one on a different day so that there is no mix-up in feeling at the end.

Exercise:

> *Later, take the categories that did not feel right and look them over carefully. Ask yourself the following questions about each one:*
> *What could be wrong about these goals?*
> *Have I overlooked something?*
> *Is there a whole different kind of goal I need to put under this category?*
> *Do I feel for some reason that I have to achieve these goals and can't change them?*

If the answer is yes, ask: Why?

The above sounds like a lot of work, but when you think of what can happen if you don't plan your goals carefully, you can see it's worth the time and effort. So often people have ideas about what is best for them and don't question them, but instead follow a life plan that becomes unattainable and unrealistic. Then they are disappointed and often feel they have failed in obtaining what they thought was a good goal.

Then, there are people who never have any goals but just live life from day to day, and then they are upset when they become older and haven't planned for what they need at that time. These people can often find themselves destitute, particularly in today's economy.

If you are someone who has not planned any goals in life, the following story may help you to realize that you should try to do so.

Roger was married to Laura and they had three children. Both Roger and Laura worked in good jobs and made a lot of money, which they spent lavishly. Their home was lovely, they both bought new cars every two or three years, and even the children were given the best throughout their youth. All went to college, which was paid for by their parents, and when the daughter married, she was given a very expensive wedding. During all this time, Roger had not even thought about planning for their old age. Both saved some money in IRAs at their jobs, but not very much. They put in the least amount they could because of how much money they needed to live on.

After the children graduated and went on to live their own lives, Roger and Laura decided it would be nice to buy a home in the country to go to for weekends. They found something very nice and very expensive, but because they had just taken out a second mortgage on their first home, they put a small down payment on the second home. Both had heavy debts at this time, both charged things all the time and never checked each other's spending.

After a couple of years of paying out huge interest rates, they realized that they needed to have a better plan, so they found a good financial advisor. He was astonished at the debts they were slowly paying off. Obviously, they were living way over their means and at the same time were paying off huge mortgages on both houses. Their savings were minimal, and even the little money they had put into IRAs was small compared to what they would need in ten years when they planned to retire.

The financial advisor advised them to sell both their homes right away and buy a smaller house to live in so that they could pay off a lot of their debts, and then he showed them what they would have in ten years if they continued to put so little money away for retirement. Roger and Laura were shocked and upset. They didn't want to sell either house. They loved them both and had spent a great deal of money decorating them. However, their financial advisor was firm and told them to check out his figures with someone else if they didn't believe him.

Roger and Laura did this and were told the same by the new adviser, who also couldn't believe how two well-earning professionals could have allowed their debts to accumulate to this degree.

Roger and Laura finally followed the advice, sold their homes for a lot of money, and bought a small place with just one extra bedroom. They added to their investments and hoped that in time they could afford the house in the country. It was too late for that however, as investments need years to double and triple for a better return. They ended up in their small home, never able to afford the other place in the country. Even when they retired, the cost of buying another place was way above their means. Both stopped spending too much, but it was too late.

This is a common story with many people. If both had invested twice as much when they were young and had curtailed their extravagance, they definitely could have kept the second home and moved there when they retired, with plenty of income to have a nice life. This showed a terrible lack of goal planning, and illustrates why it is so important to have goals that are attainable.

Sometimes, someone can have a goal that is simply unrealistic. If the goal is too extreme and too based on fantasy, then it will never be realized. After you have determined exactly what your long-range goal is, it is important to plan the in-between steps that need to happen first. A good example of this is the following:

Lilli was a very good musician and had studied several instruments most of her life. At this time she was twenty-two and was working in a corporation as a secretary, but she continued her musical studies hoping someday to find a job as a violinist in an orchestra.

Lilli auditioned for everything she could find, but only got one job playing for someone who was on maternity leave, and it was with a small local orchestra that did not have a great reputation. Lilli was talented, but she knew she needed to study with someone at a higher level than the teachers she had. With a lot of research, she found a very well known teacher in a nearby city, an hour commute for her. She auditioned for him and he agreed to take her on as a student. Of course, he was very expensive and her job didn't pay very much, but she was determined to study with him anyway.

Lilli literally sold everything of value she owned, and she also got a part-time job working on Saturdays. She had been living by herself in a small apartment, but, even though she hated the idea, she decided to move home with her parents because it would give her the extra money. She could also practice in the basement there, as they didn't mind.

Her parents weren't very supportive at this point. They thought it was a pipe dream and that she should save her money and go to nursing school, a career which Lilli had been interested in at one time. They could afford to help her financially but refused to do so because of how they felt. They did help by allowing her to live in their home, and they also fed her and even bought her clothes once in a while. Fortunately, they were nice people, so they left her alone to do the practicing she needed to do.

Her new teacher, Lionel, was tough and demanding. He could see that she had talent, which is why he took her on, but she hadn't learned the discipline or the skills that would strengthen her playing. When he first interviewed her, she told him that she played three instruments: the piano, the violin, and the clarinet. He asked her why she chose the violin over the other two. She explained that when she played the violin she felt it in her heart, whereas the others didn't give her that feeling. It was this answer that made him decide to take her as a student. Her technique needed to be developed, and this is what he rigorously set out to do.

In several months, her playing had improved considerably and even her parents sometimes stopped what they were doing to listen to her practice. Lionel was planning a private recital with his best students and he asked Lilli to play in it. This delighted her, as she knew the others were far more advanced than she. What she didn't know was that there was someone coming from a famous music school in New York to hear the students. Generally, they offered a scholarship to one of the students who they felt had great potential. This school produced the finest musicians in the country and guaranteed finding jobs for them in the best orchestras.

Lionel knew that Lilli was not as good technically as his other students, but when she played, her love of the music became part of the piece and made others feel the same energy in their hearts. This, he knew, was a special gift.

Because of this, Lilli was given the scholarship. She went to the famous school, graduating with high honors, but she did not take a job in an orchestra. She became so good that she was asked to play solo for major orchestras, and soon she became a famous violinist, giving concerts all over the world.

This is not a fairy tale. It took determination, dedication, hard work, and knowing in her heart that this was what she had to do. She did not let anyone or anything stop her from her dream.

The way to success of any kind always requires all four of these qualities, and not allowing the distractions of the mundane world to keep you from achieving your goal. But mainly, you need to feel the love of what you are doing in your heart. That joy gives you the impetus to move forward though the obstacles that arise. It's important to see those obstacles as challenges that can be gotten through.

When Lilli couldn't afford the lessons, she did not give up. Even when her parents offered to support her through nursing school, she was not tempted. If she had not moved in with her parents, she would have borrowed money. She would have found a way to follow through. It took courage, as well as dedication—the courage to fight anything that could stop her. This kind of energy comes from the heart.

Exercise:

> *When you have decided on the right goals for you to*
> *pursue, ask yourself the following questions:*
> *Do I have the courage to follow through on this?*
> *Do I have the proper determination to follow through?*
> *Do I have the dedication and commitment to follow*
> *through?*
> *If you say no to any of the above, ask your Higher Self:*
> *Why don't I have this concerning my goal?*
> *Do I lack this because of any childhood conditioning?*
> *If I could feel this, would any fears come up for me?*
> *If the answer is yes, ask: Why?*

As you work with your heart throughout this book, you will begin to understand how your heart can help you do anything in life. Use it wisely, but remember to use it with the determination that can help you move forward toward your goals.

25

Making the Heart Work for You in New Ways

We have covered many aspects of the heart and ways in which utilizing its energy can help you in your daily life. There are also other ways in which you can use your heart that may sound new and even strange to you. I am going to list them and then go into more detail about each item on the list later.

- Using heart energy to communicate and connect to nature.
- Using heart energy to handle other kinds of energy, both negative and positive.
- Recognizing when you are being sent heart energy.
- Using heart energy to protect yourself and the heart.
- Using heart energy to feel if you are having some problems in your body functions.
- Determining if your heart energy can be useful in a situation that is overloaded with negativity.

Take the first statement about communicating with nature. If you are someone who believes that nature is energy and that flowers and trees have beautiful vibrations, then you may like to experiment with doing some exercises to connect with what are called the nature spirits, who are in charge of the various forms in nature. If you don't have that belief, then you can bypass this.

Nature spirits are specific energy types that help the form they are in to grow and flourish. For example, a flower has a nature spirit in charge of helping all the parts of the flower grow from a seed to a flower. Each part has sparks of energy that are sometimes called elementals, just like people have DNA that forms and helps the function of our human systems. These elementals are governed by the nature spirit of the plant and stay active with the plant until it dies, at which time the nature spirit goes on to another new budding plant. In nature, a tree, a plant, a bush, everything that changes and grows has this system. Some sensitive humans can feel the nature spirits and their energy, and others can even communicate with them. This is always done by linking with your heart and using your heart energy to connect. The method of doing this is the following:

Exercise:

> *Pick a plant, a flower, a tree, or anything that you feel is very beautiful. Sit down in front of it, connect with your heart, and then send your heart energy to the nature spirit in it. As you send the energy, ask the spirit if you may communicate with it. If your heart has a good response, then stay with the form you have chosen. If you feel nothing in your heart, or even a resistance in it, then choose some other form. There are nature spirits that are friendly to humans and others that are not, which is why you need to stay with one you can positively communicate with.*
>
> *If you feel a response, tell the nature sprit that you feel it is very beautiful, compliment it, and then ask if it would tell you something about itself. You may suddenly have a thought come into your mind, or you may even feel something in your body that conveys something. If you are not certain that what you receive is correct and not made up, tell the nature spirit what you received and ask it to show you a response that this was correct. A proper response would be that a leaf or a flower would move even though no wind is present, or you may suddenly feel warmth in your heart.*

This is an exercise that takes time to work. Keep asking the same nature form, but if you feel nothing is happening, move to another form and try working with that. It really takes practice, mainly because the nature spirits are not used to humans talking with them. They hear your thoughts and words as vibrations, and they can return vibrations that then translate into words. Once you have made that connection, then it becomes easier. Always tell the form it is beautiful and thank it for communicating with you. Say you hope to talk with it again and try to follow through with that.

Take the second statement about handling energy. This book has talked about energies and how there are negative and positive vibrations of energy that surround all situations. For example, if you walk into a room in which some people have been fighting, the anger vibrations can fill the room and make it feel very negative. The same is true if you are in a chapel in which people have been praying for years, the positive energy in such a setting can also be felt. In both instances, the energy floods the area and can have effects on those who enter it.

In the example of negative energy, when you enter such an area and feel the negative vibrations, your response may be negative, as you are picking up those vibrations. Or, you can step back, recognize what is there, and use your heart energy to try to change the energy to something more positive.

Exercise:

> *Link with your heart and imagine that positive energy*
> *is flowing from your heart around the room. Literally*
> *see every corner of the room and its walls, then move*
> *the energy inward, to the furniture and the air around*
> *the furniture, and continue sending energy from your*
> *heart. End by saying to yourself, "May my heart energy*
> *flow throughout this whole room and change its energy*
> *to a positive one."*

Then leave the room for a while, and upon returning, feel how it feels. Sometimes doing this will clear up all the negative vibrations and it will feel fine, but sometimes the negativity is too strong. If that is the case, you may have to burn sage or incense to clean the room further.

If you enter a room in which the positive vibrations are too much and feel overwhelming, it is important to link with your heart and ask your heart energy to disperse the vibrations throughout the room in a way that keeps them positive but not overwhelming. This rarely happens, but there have been incidents where positive vibrations have made someone faint in ecstasy, leading the person to believe he has had a profound mystical experience, when it was mainly an experience of taking in too many positive vibrations. Mystical experiences certainly contain positive vibrations, but these never make anyone faint as a result.

Take the third statement about recognizing when you are being sent heart energy. This concerns your receptivity. When someone you love and who loves you thinks about you with love in his heart, you can literally feel that love coming to you. The same is true when you are thinking about the person and sending him love. This is a communication of energy. Often, when this happens, the recipient will suddenly think about the person who is sending the love, and even respond by calling the person and saying how he was thinking about her, and the other person will then similarly respond. This often happens in close-knit relationships, such as parents with their children, and with lovers. Basically, it's all about sending heart energy. You can even make yourself more receptive than you are now by doing the following exercise:

Exercise:

> *Link with your heart and ask your Higher Self the following:*
> *Has anyone sent me love today?*
> *If the answer is yes, ask: Who was it?*
> *If you receive a name of someone, put that person's*
> *name into your heart and send love back to that person.*

Try doing this at the end of the day. If you keep getting the same name given to you, then you may want to get in touch with the person and say that you have been thinking about him, and ask if anything is wrong or if he needs something. This is because sometimes if someone is thinking about you on a regular basis, it can be simply that they need help and don't know how to ask you for it.

Fine-tuning your heart so you can pick up things more easily is a positive heart action to work on. Again, it is about doing these exercises to help develop those abilities.

Take the fourth statement about protecting yourself and your heart. This refers to someone who is very sensitive and picks up vibrations and is affected by them. This kind of person is super body sensitive and can feel the vibrations penetrate his body. If the vibrations are negative, it can make this person ill. If they are positive, the vibrations can cause a feeling of being overwhelmed and therefore too vulnerable. Such a person needs to learn to protect his body and his heart, which experiences the vibrations first. Sometimes, if a person is too sensitive, he has to live in the country, as living in a city with all types of people emitting all types of vibrations will have a negative effect on him. This person cannot be around negative people, or even someone who has high positive energy, as it can flood him.

Vibrations can affect even people who do not have this problem when they occur suddenly and the person's natural protective mechanisms are not prepared. Generally, these people can handle vibrations of any kind because there is a built in protection in their body that will block too many vibrations from entering it. But if the vibrations happen too quickly and the defenses aren't up, the person can feel flooded.

If this happens to you, it is necessary to immediately do the following:

Exercise:

> *Link with your Higher Self and ask that it put armor around your body and a special shield of protection in front of your heart that can open. When you feel better and are not feeling overwhelmed and vulnerable, then lift the heart shield and ask your heart to send positive energy out into the room if the energy there is negative. If there is too much positive energy, just keep the shield closed until you feel yourself again, and only then open the shield and let some of the positive energy come into your heart. Feel your heart contain it, and only then take your armor off slowly. But if you again start to feel overwhelmed, put the armor back on.*

If you learn to protect yourself, you do not need to live in the country. You can live in the city, but make certain that if you are sensitive, you put your armor on. If, in that process, you talk with someone who is positive, then you can open the shield so your heart energy flows naturally. Only close that shield when you feel negative vibrations in the area or from the person with whom you are talking. This is for those who are supersensitive.

Take the fifth statement about using heart energy to determine if you are having body problems. This concerns being more aware of your health and how your body is feeling in all its functions. People who have little recognition of what is going on in their bodies really need to develop the ability to be more in touch with what is happening. The best way of doing this is by using the heart energy to check it out. For example, someone is feeling very tired and exhausted but will keep working on something until his exhaustion makes him ill. This person does not listen to any signs his body is sending him. Instead of stopping the work, he pushes his body until it collapses. Then he may be ill for several days. Instead, had he rested when he needed to, he would not have ended up in bed. The same is true with someone who has signs of an illness coming on but completely ignores them. He may be feeling that he is getting a cold, but he ignores it and goes out without warm enough clothing on. There are a lot of examples of people who never pay attention to what is happening physically, and, as a result, some of these people have became seriously ill or have died. If you are someone who fits this description, please do the following exercise:

Exercise:

> *Ask your Higher Self the following questions:*
> *How can I be more aware of something going wrong in my body?*
> *Is there anything that is preventing me from being more aware?*
> *If the answer is yes, ask: What is it?*
> *What would be a good daily routine for me to check how my body is functioning?*
> *If I were experiencing something happening in my body, what would be the best thing for me to do next?*
> *Is there anything preventing me from doing this?*
> *If the answer is yes, ask: What is it?*

Essentially, the body is an extension of your mind and heart. The physical mind and heart are the primary movers of all the functions. If something were going wrong, both would know what it is. It would be good, once in a while, to check in with both and ask how your body is doing and if there is anything wrong that you need to know about. You do this by taking a minute to first link with your heart and put into it the question, "How is my body functioning?" If a feeling comes up that it is okay, put that into your mind and think, "It's okay." If your mind has another thought, then put that thought back into your heart and again feel if that thought is correct. If you get a feeling that it is not okay, ask your mind what to do and put that answer into your heart for a confirmation.

Take the last statement about whether you use heart energy in a situation that is overloaded with negativity. In general, you always try to send positive energy into a room or area that you feel has a lot of negativity, but there may be times when the area is so full of negativity that any energy you send would be immediately overpowered by the negative vibrations. It's best, then, to simply leave the place if you can, but if you can't, then it's best to immediately put armor around your body and heart to protect yourself.

Sometimes it's difficult to determine what the best action is. The following are some ways you can assess how to proceed:

- If an argument is occurring, first try to talk calmly with the participants, but if they won't listen, then withdraw.

- When you enter a room and feel the negative vibrations, ask your Higher Self how powerful these vibrations are. Also ask: Is it possible to use my heart to change them? If the answer is no, that's not possible, then protect yourself or leave if you can.

- You enter someone's home and it is disorderly and full of clutter. It would be impossible to change the vibrations until the place were cleaned up. Just protect yourself and try to leave as quickly as possible.

- There is a negative situation between two people that continues without change. They are stuck in a karmic pattern, and it is too difficult to leave. This is their problem, so try not to interfere. Simply protect yourself from the negativity.

- You are traveling and have a hotel room that is full of negative vibrations. Burn some incense or sage, and if you are a person who meditates, immediately meditate and ask that your heart send positive vibrations throughout the room. If this doesn't seem to change the vibrations, try to change the room, and if that is not possible, protect yourself at all times when you are there.

There may be other times when you feel uncertain if your heart energy would help in a situation. When there is doubt, always link with your heart and ask your Higher Self what to do. It knows immediately what the best action is.

Heart energy has a wide range of uses. This book has covered many of them, but you will find as you work with it on your own that there may be some more ways that affect you directly. The beauty of working with the heart is that it is always changing and always bringing deeper understanding into your consciousness. Be open to that happening in your life.

26

Seeing the Planet with the Heart

This chapter is about expanding the heart energy to encompass not only yourself and those around you, but also using heart energy to help the planet.

If you look at energy of any kind, it is never enclosed but flows from one place to another. Energy is a vibration that can be either positive or negative depending on the sender. If you send love to someone, you are sending positive energy from your heart. If you are sending hate toward someone, the energy then becomes very negative. The same is true with what is happening on the planet. If one culture hates another culture, then there is war, destruction, and many other terrible expressions of hatred. The opposite is also true; if there is cooperation and helpfulness between nations, that energy is positive and can carry good and lasting vibrations.

As an individual, you also can send positive vibrations to those people who are suffering and need help. People can help financially, but sending positive energy is also a wonderful act of kindness.

In your daily practice, add the following exercise.

Exercise:

> *Take a minute to look at what is happening on the planet. Choose a place where you know there is a lot of suffering. It can be a place where there have been recent natural disasters, such as earthquakes, or it can be a*

*place where you know there are vast amounts of poverty
and even destruction because of wars. When you have
chosen a place, put it into your heart and ask if this
place is the one you need to work with. If you feel it's not
right, then choose another area.*

*When you finally have the right one, try to visualize
the place and the people in it. You may even want to
research it on the Internet before doing the exercise. Try
to feel what it would be like to walk down a street there.
What are the living conditions? How do the people
feel? Really let yourself become part of the scene. Then,
again, link with your heart and say, "May my heart
energy flow into this place and help the people there
and also help heal any of the elementals that have been
disturbed there." Try to feel the energy flowing from
your heart to that destination.*

*If you are going to a scene where there has been a disas-
ter, such as an earthquake, you can also ask that you be
of help to those who have died and need help to go on.*

Many people who have died suddenly do not realize that they are dead
and will linger around their homes. They then need to be helped over to
the light.

This is a simple exercise, but one that can really be helpful. Your energy
can literally go there and help. If a group of people do this, the energy becomes much stronger.

Too often people feel they can't make a difference when that is not
true. Even a child praying for people who are hurt in an earthquake will
sooth someone who is suffering. Positive thought can travel vast distances,
especially when it originates in the heart.

You may or may not believe you can do this. The main thing is to try
it, and try to feel the energy moving through your heart when you do this
work.

The following story happened to a friend of mine:

Lillian was working with a teacher on learning how
to use her heart energy properly. She was a very warm-
hearted person who tried to love everyone, but she
lacked discrimination in using her heart energy. Her
teacher explained the difference between just want-

ing to love someone and wanting to use heart energy to help someone. The first was coming from her heart naturally, and the second needed training in how to do it properly. This concept was very difficult for her to understand.

"When I simply love someone, isn't that energy helpful?" she asked him.

"Not necessarily. If the person needs to understand a problem, just sending her love won't help. It could also burden her. Working with just the heart energy is different. It could be that the person needs you to listen and reflect back to her so that she can go deeper in her probing around the problem."

"But how can I do that when I normally would just send love?"

"In your case, you need to learn to control your heart energy more by asking your Higher Self the best way to do this."

Lillian's Higher Self told her that the way for her to control her heart energy was to put a shield over her heart when she talked with a person for whom she felt a lot of love. Before meeting with her loved one, she needed to connect and send her heart energy through her Higher Self, asking it to send the energy to the other person's Higher Self, to be given to her loved one when it could help her the most and in the right manner. The Higher Self also explained that it would be better for her to do this when she was not talking with the person, as her tendency to send love might come in strongly. That was why she needed to shield herself when she was in the person's presence.

Lillian worked on doing this, but she found it much too difficult when she was with David, a man she cared about. To withdraw from reaching out to him felt too wrong to her. She again went to her teacher for help, and he asked her to meditate on why she was having so much trouble.

When she meditated, she saw a scene of a past life in which David was her child and the child died in her

arms from an illness she could not prevent. Knowing
this information helped her to understand her great
need to help him with love.

It still took time for her to learn to control her
heart energy and learn how to direct it to others without the normal feeling of love.

When you start working with using your heart energy to help others
and to send it to other places, it may seem strange to you that the energy is
not love energy but a much higher energy that flows to the areas that need
it the most. The kind of energy you are sending across the planet consists
of many elements. Usually, love heart energy is personal. Sending heart
energy to people on the planet is never personal and is much stronger because there are no attachments connected to it. In the previous example,
Lillian was told to use the Higher Self to filter the right kind of energy to
David. This is because of her personal attachment to him, but, generally,
when you have no knowledge of the people, there are no attachments, so
the heart energy can be sent directly.

If you are sending energy to someone you know, it's always best to do
this by going through your Higher Self to the other person's Higher Self.
If the person is not ready to receive it, then her Higher Self won't let it
through until she is more open to it. When you do this, let her Higher Self
decide the right type of energy she needs.

Sometimes when you are sending heart energy to other places, feelings
and even fears may arise. The following are some reasons this can happen.

- Sending it to a culture with which you have old connections.
- Wanting the energy to really work, but doubting yourself.
- Having a sudden fear around the place.
- Looking at the planet and never feeling connected to any place and not knowing why.
- Seeing yourself as not sending the right kind of energy that could be helpful.
- Not feeling dedicated to doing this type of work.
- Wanting to follow through but always forgetting to do so.
- Seeing yourself as weak-willed and therefore incapable of doing it.

- Hoping to experience more than you do.
- Coming back to where you are physically and so stopping the sending.

All of these are genuine things that can come up for people and sometimes prevent them from trying to do the work.

Exercise:

> *If any of the first nine reasons hold true to you, take the statement and ask your Higher Self the following questions:*
> *Why do I feel this way?*
> *Does this feeling in anyway originate in my childhood conditioning?*
> *If you believe in past lives, ask if this feeling comes from past lives.*
> *How can I change this feeling to a more positive one?*

If you know a specific organization that does work that interests you and that you feel is helping the planet, then consider joining the group and volunteering to help in their programs. Such help is always needed. There are many organizations now whose purpose is to help people of different cultures and religions live in peaceful coexistence, with the goal to put an end to conflicts that cause more separation and prejudice. There are also many organizations that provide basic needs in third world countries. All of this work is heart based and hopefully someday will bring about a planet of wholeness.

If you find resistance to any of these questions, go deeper and ask why you are feeling this.

On the tenth reason, try not to be too hard on yourself. It is very normal to go back and forth in the beginning stages. If you find you are back physically and out of the scene, try to refocus and go right back. All of this takes practice, and going back to the scene can happen very easily. If you can't return, then wait until the next day and try it again.

Seeing the planet with the heart also refers to something quite different from the above exercises.

Exercise:

> *Ask yourself: Do I want to in any way help or volunteer for an organization that is doing work to help the planet?*
> *If the answer is yes, ask your Higher Self: What would be the best way to do this?*
> *If the answer is no, ask your Higher Self: Is there something else that would be better for me to do?*

When you start to see the planet with your heart, you may also start seeing how nature is being affected on our planet. If this is an area in which you are most interested, ask yourself if there is anything you can do to be of help. Sometimes, you may simply protest when the government is not properly passing legislation that will protect the environment, or you may want to be more active in your community. There are youth organizations that are working to educate teenagers about ecology and how to improve their environment. These groups are springing up in many communities and schools throughout the country. There is one in my community called Greenagers that does wonderful work.

Using the heart in nature is not only talking with the nature spirits but also taking a stand to protect nature from being destroyed by the modernization that is happening. Think about what you may want to do to keep nature beautiful, as humankind has destroyed so much. We have cut down forests, affecting the wild life that lives there; we have polluted our oceans and waters with oil spills and much more. The heart of nature and its beauty is being lost, and it may become worse for future generations if something is not done to stop it.

If you see the planet with your heart, you may see many inequities. It will take time to solve many of those, but one step at a time can eventually make a difference. The heart feels these because of its connection to the feminine, which is the source of nature itself. Use your heart to see our planet, use it to feel the planet and how it is evolving. You are part of its evolution.

Exercise:

> *Ask your Higher Self: How can I use my heart to best understand the evolution of this planet?*
> *Is there anything I need to do to help in that evolution in any way?*

Take both answers and ask for a process and a first step in doing this.

When you look at life in the world and the living conditions in most parts of the planet, and when you look at nature and how its beauty is being destroyed, try to understand with your heart how you can help in even a small way.

There is a saying in the East: "If I had a dollar, I would spend fifty cents for a loaf of bread to feed my body and fifty cents for a flower to feed my soul."

27

Finding Your Truth with the Heart

When a person has opened the heart, it brings him a sense of a whole being, a being not just of a personality but a being connected to all of life. It is through this knowledge that one can go more deeply within and find what is often talked about as "be-ness."

This be-ness is a state in which the individual can feel serene and even content, whether he is going through troubles or feeling a lot of joy in his daily life. To be in this state and remain there requires an open heart that can handle the many types of energies that surround one's daily life.

For instance, if a person is in a stressful situation, he can go through that situation with no attachments and remain always calm and in full control of his mind and feelings. Such a person can handle crises without falling apart, because the inner place in which he is usually dwelling gives him an understanding that no matter what happens to him, it can never affect who he really is.

When someone has achieved that place of being, it helps those around him, for they can feel his tranquility and also can trust in his ability to do what is right. Part of opening the heart is finding discrimination and being able to understand the right way to handle anything. Such discrimination is an energy that comes through the heart and is sometimes thought about as an inner knowing. The following story is an example of this:

Ashley, an older woman in her late sixties, lived alone in an apartment in a major city. Her family was spread out across the country and consisted of three children, two boys and one girl, all with grown up families. Her husband had died recently and she was still feeling the loss, as they were very close.

One day when she was walking down the street, an elderly man in front of her was suddenly attacked by a thief and knocked down. She called for help as she ran to him, but no one heard her and she didn't have her cell phone with her. When she kneeled down next to him, she saw that he was unconscious and bleeding profusely.

She ran into the street, threw up her arms, and could have easily been hit by an oncoming car, but the driver fortunately saw her in time and stopped. She screamed at the driver to call for help and then ran back to the man. Without thinking, she ripped off her blouse and tied a bandage around his bleeding head and around his arm, which was also bleeding. She then sat on the pavement and started to calmly talk to him, saying it would be all right, that he was going to be all right, over and over again in an almost lyrical manner.

An ambulance arrived and she accompanied him to the hospital. She told the emergency room doctor what had happened and waited until he told her that the man had a concussion but would be fine. Only then did she realize that she didn't have her purse and that she must have dropped it when she ran into the street. The police were at the hospital taking a report, and they gave her money to take a taxi home. When she arrived there, her doorman said that a woman came by and gave him her handbag. Her address had been inside it.

During this whole time, Ashley was calm and connected to her heart. She felt no emotions surrounding her actions. She just knowingly did what her heart told her. It was as if she were following an inner direction that was not connected to her personality. Instead, it was instinctually coming from a source that is within all people.

When she went to visit the man later to check on his condition, he told her that even though he was unconscious, he was aware of her voice soothing him and it made him feel that he would survive. They remained friends for many years after this.

I'm certain you may know stories like Ashley's, about people doing heroic acts without thinking about their own welfare. These stories always touch a person's heart because they show how an ordinary person can find outstanding courage to respond in times of crisis.

Let's look at some ways in which you can discover who you are, not in terms of your personality, but in terms of your essence of being. Some of these might be:

- Knowing the right action to take at a critical time.
- Feeling within a connection to something beyond your understanding.
- Having an understanding of someone not based on knowledge.
- Looking beyond what you have learned.
- Having an inner knowing about something about which you have no mental knowledge.
- Feeling you can do something that you never had thought you could do.
- Having to make a sudden decision and it comes quickly from a hidden source within.
- Hoping to fulfill a task but having no attachment to doing so.
- Knowing when to stop a process that you are into.
- Feeling no attachment to those you love.
- Feeling no attachment to success of any kind.
- When you have personal needs that are not being fulfilled, having the ability to let them go without regret.
- Seeking wisdom.
- Finding yourself separate but not alone.

- Looking at reality in a unique way.

- Observing life around you in a manner that is more intro-spective.

- Knowing there is something mysterious you don't under-stand but which you hope to discover more about.

- When you find something you do not understand, you can accept it on its own terms.

- Feeling there is more to life than you have discovered.

- Hoping to delve more deeply into the philosophies of the Divine.

Exercise:

> *Go through the list above and rate yourself from one to ten, ten being the one you feel you have the most. Then add any other statement to the list that you feel has not been expressed. Prioritize the list, putting the ones you feel you have most at the top. Then, taking each one, ask your Higher Self the following questions:*
> *When I am feeling this, am I aware of that feeling?*
> *If the answer is no, ask: How can I be more aware of it?*
> *When I feel this, is there an action I need to take that I am not aware of?*
> *If the answer is yes, ask: What is it?*
> *Does this come up for me often?*
> *If the answer is yes, ask: Is there a reason for this?*
> *Am I aware that this feeling goes beyond my personal-ity?*
> *If the answer is no, ask: Why not?*
> *Am I in any way not using my inner resources?*
> *If the answer is yes, ask: Why is that?*

Sometimes a person operates from a place within that he is not aware of. Life is a constant stream of events that often leaves no time for real in-trospection. To discover your be-ness you need to take time to probe more deeply inside yourself.

Exercise:

Ask yourself the following questions:
Taking a resolved situation or problem, ask: Was there a solution to this that may have had a better outcome?
Is there something inside me that can help me on a different level that I am not aware of?
Do I try to follow the outcome of any action, or do I simply follow the solution that comes up for me?
How deeply do I go within when I want to gain a better understanding of someone?
When I follow a plan, do I adjust it in the process according to what is happening at the time?
How often do I plan steps to the final outcome?

People in general take action without looking at the consequences of those actions, mainly because they are not using their heart to go further within for a deeper understanding. They base their actions on what they know rather than who they are.

Exercise:

Link with your heart and ask yourself the following questions:
When I choose an action, do I take time to check it out with my heart?
If the answer is no, ask: How can I remember to do this?
When I remember to link with my heart, do I then remember to take the information to my mind and bring the answer back to my heart to deepen the understanding?
If the answer is no, ask yourself: How can I remember to do this?
When I think about myself, do I think mainly about my accomplishments or do I go deeper and think about who I really am as a person?
Every time I link with my Higher Self, do I feel its essence and know that this is what I can obtain?
When I look at the people I am close to, do I see them for their be-ness or do I see them for their accomplishments?

When I think about life in general, do I feel that all
people have some same quality within which unites
them as humans?
If I seek something more spiritual within myself, do I
seek it with an open mind and heart?

When a person is striving to find who he is, many things that he never knew about himself can appear. Some of those things can be negative and some positive. When something within is revealed, there can arise problems of discernment. For example, if someone feels he is working hard at finishing a difficult process, but midway discovers flaws in the initial work and therefore has to stop and start the process all over again, does that person do so with anger in his heart? Or does he have the ability to learn from his mistake and go through the process positively?

When things become difficult, they always become challenges for the individual to work through. Some people will accept the challenges and move through them quickly, whereas others will become stuck and go to a place within that is negative.

Exercise:

Ask yourself the following questions. Be honest in your
evaluations of yourself.
When faced with a difficult decision to make, do I ap-
proach it with a positive attitude?
If I am in a situation that needs direction, can I do this
with a warm heart even when it means I must be open
and kind to someone I dislike?
Am I governed by my emotions when I make important
decisions?
Do I understand my true motives around an issue that
needs resolving?
Can I be fair-minded when dealing with someone I do
not like?
If I discover a negative trait I have, do I try to change it?
When I look at the people I love, can I see them with
true discrimination or can my observation be clouded?
Am I ever retrospective?
Can I be openhearted during the most difficult times?
Can I be fair in my judgments during the most difficult
times?

These are just some questions to ask yourself that help you to come to a clearer understanding of who you are. If you receive a negative response to any of the above questions, take the answer and ask your Higher Self why you feel this way. If you then want to change this, ask the Higher Self to give you a process and a first step in changing it.

Most people never think about how their actions affect and influence others. When someone does an action, he creates energy that flows outward. This energy is within the action itself and affects the receivers as well as the end result of its manifestation. Each positive step along the way helps to make the energy pure in its flow. The most important step is the inner heart work, where true knowledge of all that needs to happen resides. When this step is eliminated, it can cause the energy to divert and not fulfill its intentions.

An example is someone who decides to start a project and jumps into the work without considering how the project will affect others, his surroundings, and himself. It may be a project that will touch many people, or just a few, but in both instances there can be ramifications that will come back to him even when he is not part of the final work.

If time were spent on each step along the way to verify the correct direction and outcome, then mistakes would not happen. The following story is an example of this:

> In Eastern Europe during the time of Charlemagne (a German Emperor born in 742), there lived at court a very learned man named Wernher, who was Charlemagne's advisor. Wernher helped plan Charlemagne's campaigns and was instrumental in his success by most carefully discerning the outcome of each action. Although Wernher's work took much longer than the work of the other advisors, Charlemagne knew that it was the best thought out, not only in terms of the route to take, but also in terms of the people they would be encountering.
>
> Charlemagne was planning a major campaign into Francia (France) in the Basque region. With Wernher's help, it was carefully strategized with all possible outcomes considered. The people there were very loyal and devoted to their lord who was in charge of the area, so Charlemagne and Wernher knew any move to conquer them would be fought with great intensity.

Wernher, after careful consideration, advised Charlemagne to change his plans and go through northern Francia, which was not as loyal and therefore would be less resistant.

Going that way would require a much longer time on the road, and so Charlemagne's other advisors made many objections. They felt that Charlemagne was so well known that even in the Basque region the people would give in right away. Wernher objected, but he was so outnumbered that he finally resigned from his position and returned home. This angered Charlemagne, and he resolved to punish Wernher on his return.

The campaign went smoothly at first. Towns fell easily, until they arrived at the main towns with the local lord's supporters. There they encountered every type of resistance and had to fall back for several days to recoup. Many men were killed on both sides, more than on any other campaigns. Charlemagne considered what to do and desperately missed Wernher advising him. When he spoke to other officers, they all felt the only thing to do was to withdraw, find more troops, and do another onslaught. Going the northern route would now be even more difficult, as it meant retracing a lot of ground that had been covered. Conditions were worsening and to go north meant finding more supplies and clothing, as the weather would be turning colder.

Instead, they recruited more men and attacked again, only to be again defeated. The townsmen were tough farmers who had all kinds of weapons that were not seen before in battle. Charlemagne's men were mostly on horseback, but the loyalists ran in and out with such dexterity that the horses could not be properly positioned. The loyalists would stab the horses' rears to make them buck and throw off their riders. Then, as soon as a rider fell, he was stabbed or hacked to death.

Charlemagne withdrew, this time back to Germany. Not only had he been defeated for the first time, but he also realized that, in his haste, he had not taken Wernher's advice to spend time deciding what his heart said about it. He had given up a plan, which, although it would have taken longer, would have given him time to win the people over and would have given him credibility and honor.

Now, because of the bravery of the loyalists, the news had spread throughout Francia and new groups of loyalists were made that would continue to fight against Charlemagne. His plan to conquer Francia was put aside until a much later time, when he was much more careful to spend the time needed to win the people over. Charlemagne never punished Wernher but apologized to him for not realizing how important it was to look at all aspects of what could happen. From then on, he did.

When you really start to work with your heart on a regular basis, you will begin to realize how many of the things that used to bother or irritate you no longer do. It's as if those minor things fall away because they can no longer impact you. Heart energy can easily discard them. There comes a time when you start to appreciate what the really important things are in your life, the things that give you joy, love, and a sense of inner well being.

You will also begin to understand how the negative emotions hold you back and never help you. The more you say no to those emotions, the more positive you feel about who you are. This be-ness is deep within, but it can become part of your consciousness, a part that makes your heart feel whole.

In working with this book, remember to take your time, going one step at a time. Like the hare and the tortoise, you will find that slow and steady perseverance is the best course and leads to an awakening of your true self.

Working With the Higher Self

The Higher Self is a part of you. It is the Wise Being within that is an accumulation of all of your positive characteristics. The energy of the Higher Self is personified in a form, which often appears as a woman or man. The gender does not have to relate to the gender of the person contacting it.

The Higher Self can also take on the form of an angel, a mystical animal, a light, a color or even an energy experienced in the body. The most common form is human, which is why in all of these exercises I will mention seeing the Higher Self as a figure, but for you the figure may just be a shaft of bright light and that is perfectly fine.

In doing the exercises, be aware that everyone is unique and experiences visualization differently. Some people can see the scenes in their mind's eye, whereas others will just feel or sense what's happening. There are also people who are auditory: they hear sounds and voices. Some will experience a combination of sensory impressions. Therefore, when you communicate with the Higher Self, it may send you impressions that appear as thoughts in your mind or you may hear its voice. It can also send body sensations that relay messages.

Sometimes personal desires can interfere with the message. Therefore, I recommend having the answer come by the use of signals. For instance, if you see the Higher Self, ask it to show you a visual signal for "yes," "no" and "maybe." A "yes" and "no" signal may simply be the shaking of its head "yes" or "no." If you have more body awareness, you may feel a twitch in your left leg for a "yes" answer, and a "no" may be a twitch in your right leg. Ask your questions accordingly. Then you can ask the Higher Self to tell you more and receive that either verbally or through impressions.

The Higher Self will always reach you in some manner. If you haven't received actual answers to your questions, the signal method is another way of communicating. Since the Higher Self is your wise Self and is part of you, it knows everything about you and everything about your personal evolution. It therefore can help you in all of your life's problems, from the most mundane to the most profound. Utilizing it to help you makes it stronger, until you begin to bring the Higher Self totally into your consciousness in your everyday life. Eventually, you will not even see a form but simply feel it in your body as being one with you. Remember, its role is not only to help you with problems, but also to guide you spiritually so that you become a wise being in all your thoughts and actions.

Because it is the Higher Self, the more you use it, the stronger is the pull of the shadow side of the personality. Consequently, the shadow side, which is also part of you and part of the unconscious, will begin to fight back in a negative manner. Be aware that you may suddenly have dark thoughts and feelings that you have never experienced before. Try to see them in a disidentified manner, and literally see them as a black ball, which you will give to your Higher Self to transmute.

Working with the Higher Self is a process. There will be times when you experience it fully in the meditation and other times when nothing happens. When first contacting the Higher Self, it can be very evasive. It may appear and then quickly disappear. The more you persist in contacting it, the stronger it will become. If it should disappear when you are communicating with it, just link with your heart center (a center located in the middle of your chest), repeat the end of the meditation, and literally demand that it return.

In all Higher Self meditations, I mention shining light on the Higher Self when you first experience it. Sometimes desires coming from your personality will impersonate the Higher Self. Shining light on it will verify it. When the rays of light shine on the Higher Self, if it is truly the Higher Self, it will either stay the same or get brighter. If it is something else, it will disappear or turn dark. If this happens, and it usually happens to everyone at some time or other, simply tell it to leave and repeat the end of the exercise. If during the exercise you experience blocks or fears, see these as a black ball, which you give to your Higher Self, saying, "Please take these away from me temporarily, so that I can receive clear answers from you."

After doing this, again shine light down on the Higher Self to be certain it is still the Higher Self. I recommend doing this at least once during the communication, just in case some inner desire has replaced the Higher Self.

If you only experience body impressions of the Higher Self, always keep connecting with the heart center. The Higher Self should convey a warm, expansive feeling. It's energy is never cold, so if you are experiencing a sudden cold feeling in the chest, reconnect with your heart center and ask the Higher Self to come back.

Working with the Higher Self is always a wonderful experience. Its wisdom and humor make a magical combination. Sometimes it will take on other forms to indicate something you need to do. For example, it may appear as a frolicking child or elf, indicating you need to have more fun or play with your inner child. It will even take on other nationalities and appear in different genders. If it suddenly changes from what you are used to seeing, ask it why it has taken on this new form.

It will sometimes appear as one of your past lives, usually a life that was deeply spiritual, like a monk or lama.

Sometimes the Higher Self will play games with you. For example, it may show you a symbol that you don't understand. It's important, then, at a later time, to take the symbol and visualize it in your heart center and ask to see or receive more information about it.

The Higher Self always works with your whole being. It will never reveal information to you that you are not ready to receive. It will never hurt you or scare you. It is gentle and loving at all times. It always knows what's best for you and it will never deceive you. If that ever happens, be aware that it's coming from something other than your Higher Self.

These exercises will introduce you to your Higher Self. The more you work with the Higher Self, the easier it becomes to contact it. You may then eliminate most of the exercise and start with a point toward the end. With some people, the Higher Self will appear just by linking with the heart center. Remember, it always operates through the heart.

The more you use your heart center in your everyday life, in all your relationships and with yourself, the stronger the Higher Self will become. You will find your heart opening and your feelings toward others becoming more compassionate. These are not sentimental feelings, but strong, simple feelings of genuine love.

Everyone is capable of opening their heart and becoming one with their Higher Self, but it requires discipline and practice. It is an ongoing process, which develops one's spiritual nature. When blocks and fears arise, as they surely will, look at them as obstacles you need to work through. Break down the fears and see the root of them. Ask for a process from your Higher Self that will help you go through the blocks, starting with a first step. Work with that step and ask for another one.

You may want to ask the Higher Self to show you a symbol, which represents it. Take the symbol of the Higher Self and draw it, keeping it in front of you during the day to remind yourself to link with the Higher Self.

Remember, the Higher Self is your inner guide; it will lead you through obstacles and help you awaken your spiritual and creative nature. Acknowledge the Higher Self when you do acts of love and kindness. We criticize ourselves when we make mistakes, but how often do we acknowledge our good qualities?

Within the Higher Self sleeps the spirit of the individual. When you activate the Higher Self, you awaken the spirit. The more you use the Higher Self to guide you in all your decisions, the more you become one with higher forces and energies. The Higher Self will help you see and transmute those characteristics which impede your spiritual growth. It takes you on the path to wholeness; it leads you to your true potential and helps you discover who you really are.

HIGHER SELF EXERCISES
Higher Self - The Mountain Exercise

Sit down in a comfortable chair.

Close your eyes and feel your whole body relaxing. First your feet are going to relax, then your legs, your thighs, your stomach, chest, shoulders and arms, your neck and head. Now your whole body is feeling relaxed.

Take some deep breaths and center yourself by linking with your heart center, which is located in the center of your chest.

With each breath, feel the cares of the day dissolving into nothing and try to let go of any thoughts and feelings.

Now imagine you are standing in a meadow and right in front of you is a mountain. You are going to climb the mountain, and it will be a very easy climb. At the very top, you will meet your Higher Self.

For now, you start to walk on the path, which is in front of you. Almost immediately you enter a forest. It's a forest of tall evergreen trees and pine. You can smell the pine, and as you walk on the path upward, you can feel the pine needles under your feet.

You can hear the birds singing and the rustle of leaves in the woods.

And as you slowly climb upward, there are rays of sunlight breaking through the branches, lighting your way.

Now you are leaving the forest and you continue climbing upward on the path. There are trees and rocks and grass, and as you climb, you can feel the warmth of the sun on your body. It's a beautiful summer day, with a gentle breeze blowing. You continue to climb upward.

Suddenly, you hear the sound of water. You leave the path, walk toward the sound and see a flowing stream of water that is gently moving downward. As some of the water hits some rocks, you feel the wet spray on your face.

You turn now and go back to the path and continue climbing upward. Now there are no more trees, just big boulders of rock, scrub brush and sand. You stop for a minute and see that there are other mountain ranges on either side. You can look down and see the meadow from where you first came.

You turn and continue climbing upward. Now you are coming to the top of the mountain, and as you go around a bend, you see at the very top a flat plateau of land, and on the plateau is a bench. Sit down on the bench and take a moment to look around you. Experience the beautiful view of mountains.

As you sit there, feel the warmth of the sun on top of your head. Now look up at the sun, which is directly above you. As you look, a figure is going to appear and slide down on a sunbeam and stand in front of you. The figure is your Higher Self. You may also experience it as a light or a feeling of warmth and expansion in your heart center. When you feel you are experiencing it, imagine the sun shining down on it and notice if it changes. If it stays the same or gets brighter, then it is your Higher Self. If it disappears or gets dark, tell it to leave and try the exercise again.

Imagine reaching out and holding the hands of your Higher Self, linking your heart to its heart. Feel its energy flowing to you. How does it feel?

When you feel connected, ask the Higher Self your questions.

Listen to its answer; it may take the form of actual words, thoughts, or impressions.

As a check for the information you've received, ask the Higher Self for signals of verification, or if there have been no direct answers, ask for signals in answer to your questions. For example, a signal for a yes answer, a no answer, or a maybe answer.

When you feel ready to end the conversation, thank your Higher Self, open your eyes and write down everything that has occurred.

Higher Self - The Meadow Exercise

Close your eyes and feel your whole body relaxing. First your feet are going to relax, then your legs, your thighs, your stomach, chest, shoulders and arms, your neck and head. Now your whole body is feeling relaxed.

Take some deep breaths and center yourself by linking with your heart center, which is located in the center of your chest.

With each breath, feel the cares of the day dissolving into nothing and try to let go of any thoughts and feelings.

Now imagine yourself standing in the middle of a meadow. It is a beautiful summer day, the sun is shining brightly and there is a soft breeze blowing.

Experience the meadow around you – the trees, the green grass with wild flowers growing, and the mountains in the distance.

You can smell the sweetness of the air and feel the warmth of the sun and the gentleness of the breeze.

You may want to take your shoes off and feel the grass under your feet.

In the distance, across the meadow, a figure appears and slowly walks toward you. You know the figure is your Higher Self. As it comes closer, try to sense what it looks like. Is it a man or a woman? Is it just a light, or is it a body feeling? The Higher Self will come to a stop in front of you.

When you feel you are experiencing it, imagine the sun shining down on it and notice if it changes. If it stays the same or gets brighter, then it is your Higher Self. If it disappears or gets dark, tell it to leave and try the exercise again.

Imagine reaching out and holding the hands of your Higher Self, linking your heart to its heart. Feel its energy flowing to you. How does it feel?

When you feel connected, ask the Higher Self your question or questions.

Listen to its answer; it may take the form of actual words, thoughts, or impressions.

As a check for the information you've received, ask the Higher Self for signals of verification. If there have been no direct answers, then ask for signals in answer to your questions.

When you feel ready to end the conversation, thank your Higher Self, open your eyes and write down everything that has occurred.

(The above two exercises are adapted material from the book Psychosynthesis, *by Roberto Assagioli.)*

Higher Self - The Garden Exercise

Sit down in a comfortable chair.

Close your eyes and feel your whole body relaxing. First your feet are going to relax, then your legs, your thighs, your stomach, chest, shoulders and arms, your neck and head. Now your whole body is feeling relaxed.

Take some deep breaths and center yourself by linking with your heart center, which is located in the center of your chest.

With each breath, feel the cares of the day dissolving into nothing and try to let go of any thoughts and feelings.

Imagine you are entering a walled garden. The entrance way has a trellis of climbing roses over it. As you enter, you see two paths. The one on the left continues to follow beds of roses. The one on the right has a variety of flowers arranged by color. Some beds are golden, full of lilies and smaller orange and yellow flowers. There are also beds of blue and purple, hyacinth and iris. Put your favorite flowers in the beds. Follow this path, which continues down to where there is a small, paved circle of stone with a bench on it. You sit down on the bench. Your Higher Self is coming down the opposite path and sits down next to you on the bench. Continue the exercise by first shining light on it.

If you choose to walk down the path of rose beds, you will see all variety and color of roses. This path also comes to the round, paved circle of stone with the bench on it, and you also see the Higher Self coming down the opposite path to sit down next to you on the bench.

When you feel connected, ask the Higher Self your question or questions.

Listen to its answer; it may take the form of actual words, thoughts, or impressions.

As a check for the information you've received, ask the Higher Self for signals of verification. If there has been no direct answer, ask for signals in answer to your questions.

When you feel ready to end the conversation, thank your Higher Self, open your eyes and write down everything that has occurred.

Higher Self - The Lake Exercise

Sit down in a comfortable chair.

Close your eyes and feel your whole body relaxing. First your feet are going to relax, then your legs, your thighs, your stomach, chest, shoulders and arms, your neck and head. Now your whole body is feeling relaxed.

Take some deep breaths and center yourself by linking with your heart center, which is located in the center of your chest.

With each breath, feel the cares of the day dissolving into nothing and try to let go of any thoughts and feelings.

This exercise is for the water lovers in the group. Pretend you are in a boat on a beautiful lake. You are rowing or paddling toward an island. You pull up to the island and dock your boat.

You get out of the boat and walk down a path that takes you to a paved pavilion that overlooks the lake. There is a bench and you wait for the Higher Self. You see it is in a boat on the lake, and it comes to a dock in front of you, gets out and meets you on the pavilion.

Shine light, and then continue the exercise.

When you feel connected, ask the Higher Self your question or questions.

Listen to its answer; it may take the form of actual words, thoughts, or impressions.

As a check for the information you've received, ask the Higher Self for signals of verification. If you have not been given any direct answers, ask for signals in answer to your questions.

When you feel ready to end the conversation, thank your Higher Self, open your eyes and write down everything that has occurred.

Higher Self - The House Exercise

Sit down in a comfortable chair.

Close your eyes and feel your whole body relaxing. First your feet are going to relax, then your legs, your thighs, your stomach, chest, shoulders and arms, your neck and head. Now your whole body is feeling relaxed.

Take some deep breaths and center yourself by linking with your heart center, which is located in the center of your chest.

With each breath, feel the cares of the day dissolving into nothing and try to let go of any thoughts and feelings.

In this exercise, imagine you are sitting in your home meditating. The doorbell rings and you go to the door and open it. On the other side is your Higher Self. It enters and sits down across from you.

Shine light and continue the exercise.

When you feel connected, ask the Higher Self your question or questions.

Listen to its answer; it may take the form of actual words, thoughts, or impressions.

As a check for the information you've received, ask the Higher Self for signals of verification. If you have not been given any direct answers, ask for signals in answer to your questions.

When you feel ready to end the conversation, thank your Higher Self, open your eyes and write down everything that has occurred.

Other Books by Nanette V. Hucknall

Karma, Destiny and Your Career

Higher Self Yoga: Book One

Higher Self Yoga: Book Two

The Rose and the Sword, co-authored with Dr. Judith Bach

Select MSI Books

Self-Help Books

A Woman's Guide to Self-Nurturing (Romer)

Anxiety Anonymous: The Big Book on Anxiety Addiction (Ortman)

Creative Aging: A Baby Boomer's Guide to Successful Living (Vassiliadis & Romer)

Divorced! Survival Techniques for Singles over Forty (Romer)

Living Well with Chronic Illness (Charnas)

Publishing for Smarties: Finding a Publisher (Ham)

Survival of the Caregiver (Snyder)

The Marriage Whisperer: How to Improve Your Relationship Overnight (Pickett)

The Rose and the Sword: How to Balance Your Feminine and Masculine Energies (Bach & Hucknall)

The Widower's Guide to a New Life (Romer)

Widow: A Survival Guide for the First Year (Romer)

Inspirational and Religious Books

A Believer-Waiting's First Encounters with God (Mahlou)

A Guide to Bliss: Transforming Your Life through Mind Expansion (Tubali)

El Poder de lo Transpersonal (Ustman)

Everybody's Little Book of Everyday Prayers (MacGregor)

Joshuanism (Tosto)

Puertas a la Eternidad (Ustman)

The Gospel of Damascus (O. Imady)

The Seven Wisdoms of Life: A Journey into the Chakras (Tubali)

When You're Shoved from the Right, Look to Your Left: Metaphors of Islamic Humanism (O. Imady)

Memoirs

Blest Atheist (Mahlou)

Forget the Goal, the Journey Counts . . . 71 Jobs Later (Stites)

Healing from Incest: Intimate Conversations with My Therapist (Henderson & Emerton)

It Only Hurts When I Can't Run: One Girl's Story (Parker)

Las Historias de Mi Vida (Ustman)

Losing My Voice and Finding Another (C. Thompson)

Of God, Rattlesnakes, and Okra (Easterling)

Road to Damascus (E. Imady)

Still Life (Mellon)

Foreign Culture

Syrian Folktales (M. Imady)

The Rise and Fall of Muslim Civil Society (O. Imady)

The Subversive Utopia: Louis Kahn and the Question of National Jewish Style in Jerusalem (Sakr)

Thoughts without a Title (Henderson)

Popular Psychology

Road Map to Power (Husain & Husain)

The Seeker (Quinelle)